The Fourteenth Amendment and the Law of the Constitution

The Fourteenth Amendment and the Law of the Constitution

Earl M. Maltz

Carolina Academic Press
Durham, North Carolina

ISBN 0-89089-232-6
LCCN 2003113290

Carolina Academic Press
700 Kent Street
Durham, NC 27701
Telephone (919) 489-7486
Fax (919) 493-5668
www.cap-press.com
Email cap@cap-press.com

Printed in the United States of America

Contents

Preface

The late nineteenth century was a critical period in the development of American constitutional law. During this period, the Supreme Court faced the task of interpreting a Constitution that had been altered by the addition of the Thirteenth, Fourteenth, and Fifteenth amendments during the early Reconstruction era. These amendments had the potential to dramatically reconfigure the structure of American constitutional jurisprudence. Against this background, the decisions reached by the late-nineteenth-century Court provided the basic premises that would govern American constitutional law well into the twentieth century, and in some cases they still have considerable influence today.

Scholarly assessments of the Court's performance during this period have varied widely. Commentators such as Pamela Brandwein, Robert J. Kaczrowski, and Harold M. Hyman and William M. Wiecek have excoriated the Court for abandoning what they see as the basic principles underlying the Reconstruction amendments in order to advance a conservative political agenda. By contrast, Michael Les Benedict has argued that many of the more conservative decisions, while perhaps not as sensitive to racial equality as one might like, were at least consistent with the basic theory of federalism shared by many of the Republicans who were responsible for drafting these amendments. However, all of these scholars proceed from the same methodological premise. Either implicitly or explicitly, they see the Republican ideology of the early Reconstruction era as the benchmark against which the performance of the Court should be measured.[1]

The difficulty with this premise is that neither the drafters nor the ratifiers of the Reconstruction amendments had the authority to enact an ideology. Instead, they simply changed the law by adding new language to the Constitution. Moreover, the language that they chose was not just political rhetoric, as William E. Nelson has contended. Nor was it distinctly associated with the antislavery movement in the nineteenth century, as Kaczrowski, Hyman and Wiecek, and Jacobus tenBroek have argued. Rather, the drafters of the amendments in general, and of section 1 of the Fourteenth Amendment in particular, took care to choose language with a well-settled meaning in American legal thought that predated the dispute over slavery and had been borrowed by both sides in that dispute.[2]

This reality informs the basic methodology of this book. Focusing on the idea that the Reconstruction amendments are in fact law, the book seeks to measure the work of the late-nineteenth-century Court against the principles of distinctively legal analysis rather than Republican ideology. The book begins with a detailed discussion of the use of Fourteenth Amendment con-

---

1. Pamela Brandwein, *Reconstructing Reconstruction: The Supreme Court and the Production of Historical Truth* (Durham, N.C., 1999); Robert J. Kaczrowski, *The Politics of Judicial Interpretation: The Federal Courts, Department of Justice and Civil Rights* (New York, 1985); Harold M. Hyman and William M. Wiecek, *Equal Justice under Law: Constitutional Development, 1835–1875* (New York, 1982); Michael Les Benedict, "Preserving Federalism: Reconstruction and the Waite Court," in Phillip B. Kurland and Gerhard Casper, eds., *The Supreme Court Review, 1978* (Chicago, 1979), pp. 39–80.

2. William E. Nelson, *The Fourteenth Amendment: From Political Principle to Judicial Doctrine* (Cambridge, Mass., 1988); Robert J. Kaczrowski, "Revolutionary Constitutionalism in the Era of the Civil War and Reconstruction," *New York University Law Review* 61 (1986): 863–939; Hyman and Wiecek, *Equal Justice under Law*; Jacobus tenBroek, *The Antislavery Origins of the Fourteenth Amendment* (Berkeley, 1951).

cepts in the antebellum era. An examination of the drafting process itself follows, documenting the claim that the drafters did indeed understand that they were choosing language with an established legal import. Finally, subsequent chapters explore the ways in which the case law of the late nineteenth century departed from these established meanings.

This project could never have come to fruition without the skills of the able secretarial staff at Rutgers Law School in Camden, New Jersey, particularly Celia Hazel and Kaeko Jackson. It was improved immeasurably by the copyediting prowess of Sherry Wert. Finally my wife, Peggy, and children, David, Elizabeth, and Jonathan are constant sources of joy and support.

Portions of this book have appeared previously in other forms. Chapter 1 is adapted from "Fourteenth Amendment Concepts in the Antebellum Era," *American Journal of Legal History* 32 (1988): 305–346. Parts of chapters 2 and 3 are taken from "The Fourteenth Amendment and Native American Citizenship," *Constitutional Commentary* 17 (2000): 555–573. Parts of chapters 4 and 5 are taken from "The Waite Court and Federal Power to Enforce the Reconstruction Amendments" in Jennifer M. Lowe, ed., *The Supreme Court and the Civil War* (Washington, D.C. 1996), pp. 75–88. Parts of chapter 6 are taken from "Only Partially Color-Blind: Justice Harlan's View of Race and the Constitution," *Georgia State Review* 12 (1996): 973–1013.

The Fourteenth Amendment and the Law of the Constitution

Chapter 1

Fourteenth Amendment Concepts in the Antebellum Era

The evolution of the Reconstruction amendments and the Supreme Court decisions interpreting those amendments can only be understood in the context of the antebellum debate over slavery and the rights of free blacks. The general constitutional theories of both antislavery and proslavery forces found expression in a variety of different legal and linguistic formulations. Among these were the three concepts that were eventually to be incorporated into section 1 of the Fourteenth Amendment—due process, equal protection, and privileges and immunities. These concepts were not, however, invented for use in the dispute over slavery; each had a well-established place in general antebellum constitutional theory. Any attempt to understand the import of the three terms must have reference to this general background, as well as to their specific applications to the issues of slavery and the rights of free blacks.

Due Process of Law

One of the most venerable concepts in American constitutionalism is the principle that persons cannot be deprived of life, liberty, or property except through the "law of the land," often described as "due process of law." Dating from the Magna Carta, this concept was embodied not only in the Fifth Amendment, but also in the antebellum constitutions of almost every state.[1] Prior to the Civil War, some states limited the due process concept to the analysis of procedural issues. In addition, however, a substantial number of states imbued their respective due process clauses with a substantive content.

In tracing the origins of the Due Process Clause, students of the history of the Fourteenth Amendment have tended to focus their attention on those cases which condemned generally the deprivation of certain vested rights. Outstanding examples are *Hoke v. Henderson*, in which the North Carolina Supreme Court struck down a statute that provided for the replacement by election of court clerks originally appointed to serve during "good behavior,"[2] and *Wynehammer v. New York*, which found unconstitutional a New York law sharply restricting the conditions under which alcoholic beverages could be stored and sold.[3] Cases such as *Hoke* and *Wynehammer* did indeed embody one important element of substantive due process analysis. However, another theme was also prominent in the first half of the nineteenth century: the rejection of "class legislation."

Apparently related to the concerns underlying the distaste for bills of attainder, condemnations of class legislation can be traced to Blackstone's definition of law itself. Law, he argued, "is a *rule*; not a transient sudden order from a superior, to or concerning a particular person; but something permanent, uniform and universal."[4] In *James v. Reynolds*, the Texas Supreme Court provided

---

1. Thomas M. Cooley, *A Treatise on the Constitutional Limitations Which Rest on the Legislative Powers of the States of the Union* (Boston, 1867), pp. 351–352.

2. 15 N.C. (4 Dev.) 1 (1833).

3. 13 N.Y. 378 (1856).

4. St. George Tucker, ed., *Blackstone's Commentaries, with Notes of Reference to the Constitution and Laws of the Federal Government of the United States and of the Commonwealth of Virginia*, 5 vols. (Philadelphia, 1803), 1:44 (emphasis in original).

a more typically American formulation of a similar principle: "The terms [*sic*] 'law of the land'...are...in their most usual acceptation, regarded as general public laws binding upon all members of the community...and not partial or private laws, affecting the rights of private individuals or classes of individuals."[5] Defending its condemnation of class legislation, the Pennsylvania Supreme Court argued:

> [W]hen, in the exercise of proper legislative powers, general laws are enacted, which bear or may bear on the whole community, if they are unjust and against the spirit of the constitution, the whole community will be interested to procure their repeal by a voice potential. And that is the great security for just and fair legislation.
>
> But when individuals are selected from the mass, and laws are enacted affecting their property, without summons or notice, at the instigation of an interested party, who is to stand up for them, thus isolated from the mass, in injury and injustice, or where are they to seek relief from such acts of despotic power? They have no refuge but in the courts, the only secure place for determining conflicting rights by due course of law.[6]

Though it figured most prominently in laws aimed specifically at individual cases, this mode of due process analysis was also occasionally used to protect small classes from discrimination. For example, in *Wally's Heirs v. Kennedy*, the Tennessee Supreme Court struck down a statute that directed the dismissal of some actions based on land claims under certain treaties with the Cherokee Indians if those claims were based on a contingent interest or prosecuted in trust for another person. While acknowledging that the

5. 2 Tex. 250, 251–252 (1852). To the same effect, see *Trustees of Dartmouth College v. Woodward*, 17 U.S. (4 Wheat.), 518, 581–582 (1819) (argument of Daniel Webster); Cooley, *Constitutional Limitations*, pp. 351–359.

6. *Ervine's Appeal*, 16 Pa. 256, 268 (1851).

statute was aimed at a genuine evil, the court held that "good cause for public indignation [did not justify] passage of a law affecting the rights of a few individuals, but by which the great body of the people, or the legislators themselves, were unwilling to be bound."[7]

The Iowa Supreme Court reached a similar conclusion in *Reed v. Wright*. There the court dealt with a territorial statute that was designed to settle claims in so-called half-breed lands. All persons having claims to such lands were required to file those claims within one year after passage of the statute. Commissioners were appointed to examine the validity of the claims, and their determination was to be binding on the courts.

The *Reed* court found the statute inconsistent with the "law of the land" provision of the Northwest Ordinance. In part, the opinion seemed to rely on procedural inadequacies of the statute; however, the concept of class legislation also played a prominent role in the court's analysis. For example, the court noted:

> Whatever might have been the exigencies which would seem to require an act to settle the different conflicting titles to the half-breed lands, still the legislature had no right... to pass a special and limited act confined to a particular class of individuals, by which they were to be deprived of their property....
>
> [The statute] is not within the scope of rightful legislation, for it does not profess to declare a general right of action for the citizen, but is partial, limited and exclusive.[8]

The scope of antebellum substantive due process analysis should not be overstated. The concept constrained only those government actions that adversely affect "vested rights." Thus, for example, legislatures were generally held free to revoke "privileges"

---

7. 10 Tenn. (2 Yer.) 554, 556–557 (1831).
8. 2 Greene 15, 27–28 (Iowa 1849).

as well as to destroy mere "expectancies." Similarly, "curative" legislation was typically held valid, notwithstanding its applicability only to small classes. In *Walpole v. Elliot*, for instance, the Indiana Supreme Court had no difficulty upholding a statute validating the proceedings of a court not held pursuant to law. Nonetheless, within the compass of vested rights, substantive due process was a significant force in antebellum jurisprudence.[9]

Opponents of slavery made frequent reference to due process arguments in their analyses. Both the procedural and substantive components of the due process concept played important roles in antislavery doctrine. In its procedural guise, the Due Process Clause figured most prominently in attacks on the Fugitive Slave Acts. Antislavery theorists contended that procedures for determining the validity of a slaveholder's claim to an alleged fugitive fell far short of constitutional minimums. Thus it was argued that blacks claimed as fugitives were being deprived of their liberty without due process of law. In *In re Booth*, the Wisconsin Supreme Court seized on this argument to justify its decision to defy federal enforcement of the Fugitive Slave Act of 1850.[10]

Substantive due process analysis played an even more prominent role in antislavery analysis. Occasionally, the Due Process Clause was invoked to protect the rights of antislavery whites. For example, in 1856, Republican Representative John A. Bingham of Ohio attacked a Kansas territorial statute that made it illegal to utter any "sentiment calculated to induce slaves to escape from the service of their masters," arguing that the statute "abridges the freedom of speech and of the press, and deprives persons of liberty without due process of law, or any process but that of brute force."[11]

---

9. 18 Ind. 258 (1862). To the same effect, see Cooley, *Constitutional Limitations*, pp. 357–358; Edwin S. Corwin, "The Basic Doctrine of American Constitutional Law," *Michigan Law Review* 12 (1914): 247–276.

10. 3 Wis. 13, 46–47 (1854). To the same effect, see Charles Sumner, "Freedom National, Slavery Sectional," in Charles Sumner, *His Complete Works* (Boston, 1870–83), 2:257–366.

11. *Congressional Globe*, 34th Cong., 1st sess., app. 124 (1856).

The most significant antislavery use of the Due Process Clause, however, was in the direct attack on the extension of slavery into the territories. As put forth by abolitionists in the 1830s and developed by Salmon P. Chase, the argument was based on the analysis of Lord Henry Mansfield in *Somerset v. Stewart.* In *Somerset,* Mansfield contended that slavery was contrary to natural law and therefore depended for its existence on the enactment of positive law by the sovereign.[12] Chase reasoned that, given this premise, slaves in the territories would become free in the absence of duly adopted federal statutes. Thus, in Chase's view, by recognizing slavery in the territories, Congress in essence deprived the slaves of their natural right to freedom. Since the slaves had committed no crimes, such a deprivation was inconsistent with the pure vested-rights concept of substantive due process. Though it never received judicial sanction, this argument formed the centerpiece of antislavery constitutional doctrine, appearing in every antislavery party platform between 1844 and 1860.[13]

The proslavery theory of substantive due process analysis was a mirror image of the antislavery position. While the antislavery forces focused on what they viewed as the natural rights of the slaves to liberty, the proslavery argument exalted the vested property rights of slaveholders. Some proslavery theorists based their due process contentions on natural law concepts of property rights; others, by contrast, relied strongly on the theme that the Constitution provided slaveholders with vested rights in this form of property.

12. Lofft 1 (K.B. 1772).

13. Salmon P. Chase, "The Address and Reply on the Presentation of a Testimonial to S. P. Chase by the Colored People of Cincinnati" (pamphlet) (Cincinnati, 1845), pp. 29–30; Liberty Party Platform of 1844, in D. B. Johnson, comp., *National Party Platforms* (Urbana, Ill., 1978), 1:5; Free Soil Platform of 1948, in ibid., p. 13; Free Democratic Platform of 1852, in ibid., p. 18; Republican Platform of 1856, in ibid., p. 27; Republican Platform of 1860, in ibid., p. 32.

These contentions recurred throughout the antebellum controversy over slavery. The proslavery forces used the Due Process Clause to buttress their arguments during the debates over the admission of Missouri in 1820, and Senators John C. Calhoun and Charles C. Pinckney of South Carolina both took the same position in 1836 while discussing slavery in the District of Columbia. For example, Pinckney's report to this issue argued that abolition in the seat of federal government would be "directly repugnant to the principles of natural justice and of the social compact" and inconsistent with the Fifth Amendment. Finally, and most notably, in *Dred Scott v. Sandford*, Chief Justice Roger Brooke Taney linked due process analysis with the state sovereignty theory to conclude that Congress could not bar slavery in the territories.[14] Often, however, the due process argument was overshadowed in proslavery theory by another principle that was later to appear in the Fourteenth Amendment—the concept of the right to equal protection of the laws.

Equal Protection of the Laws

The right to protection of the law was central to the social contract theory that dominated nineteenth-century political thought.[15] Under this theory, the right to protection by the sovereign authority is the quid pro quo that inhabitants receive for giving up some of the rights that they possess in the state of nature. In the shorthand of the era, allegiance is the obligation of the citizen, and protection the obligation of the sovereign. The alle-

14. *Annals of Congress*, 16th Cong., 1st sess., 998, 1521 (1820); *Congressional Globe*, 24th Cong., 1st sess., 81 (1836); H. R. Rep. no. 691, 24th Cong., 1st sess., 14 (1836); 60 U.S. (19 How.) 393 (1858).

15. The understanding of the right to protection of the law in the antebellum era is discussed in detail in Stephen J. Heyman, "The First Duty of Government: Protection, Liberty and the Fourteenth Amendment," *Duke Law Journal* (1991): 507–541.

giance/protection equation made early appearances in British legal materials. In 1608, Lord Coke made the reciprocal obligations of allegiance and protection an explicit point in his opinion in *Calvin's Case*. Sir William Blackstone later made much the same point, arguing that

> the principal aim of society is to protect individuals in the enjoyment of... rights, which were vested in them by the immutable laws of nature; but which could not be preserved in peace without that mutual assistance and intercourse, which is gained by the institution of friendly and social communities.

Further, he argued,

> [T]he original contract of society [is] that the whole should protect all its parts, and that every part should pay obedience to the will of the whole; or, in other words, that the community should guard the rights of each individual member, and that (in return for the protection) each individual should submit to the laws of the community.[16]

The same concepts were equally influential on the American scene. Theorists as diverse as John C. Calhoun and Francis Lieber plainly subscribed to the allegiance/protection equation. Chancellor James Kent's *Commentaries on American Law* similarly asserted that "[t]he personal security of every citizen is protected from lawless violence by the arm of the government and the... penal code," that "[e]very person is entitled to be protected in the enjoyment of his property," and that "[the] duty of protecting every man's property by means of just laws, promptly, uniformly, and impartially administered, is one of the strongest and most in-

---

16. See, for example, James H. Kettner, *The Development of American Citizenship, 1608–1870* (Chapel Hill, 1978); "Speech of Harrison Gray," in Otis Yates, *Rights of Colored Men to Suffrage, Citizenship and Jury Trial* (Boston, 1838), p. 47; *Calvin's Case*, 7 Coke 1 (1608); Tucker, *Blackstone's Commentaries*, 1:47, 124.

teresting of obligations on the part of government." Many early state constitutions identified protection of basic rights as the prime function of government.[17] Finally, early Comity Clause cases, such as *Corfield v. Coryell* and *Campbell v. Morris*, identified a right to government protection of person and property that was analytically distinct from such interests as the right to pursue lawful occupations and the right to acquire and hold real and personal property.[18]

The basic parameters of the right to protection were fairly well established in the antebellum era. Obviously, the right to protection must embrace the ability to claim protection from personal aggression by other persons within the sovereign's territory, as well as to hold property within that territory free from such aggression. The right comes most clearly into play when the gov-

17. Francis Lieber, *Miscellaneous Writings* (1880), 2:177–178; John C. Calhoun, *A Disquisition on Government*, Political Science Classics edition (New York, 1947), p. 55; James Kent, *Commentaries on American Law* (New York, 1826–30), 2:15, 331, 333–334; Iowa Constitution of 1846, art. 1, sec. 1, reprinted in William F. Swindler, *Sources and Documents of United States Constitutions* (Dobbs Ferry, N.Y., 1979), 3:434; Preamble to Massachusetts Constitution of 1780, reprinted in ibid., 5:92; Virginia Constitution of 1851, Bill of Rights, art. 3, reprinted in ibid., 10:68.

18. *Corfield v. Coryell*, 6 F. Cas. 546, 551–552 (C.C.E.D. Pa. 1823) (no. 3230); *Campbell v. Morris*, 3 H. NcH. 535, 554 (Md. 1797). In addition, see Tucker, *Blackstone's Commentaries*, 2: app. 77–79 (although slaves should be freed, they should not be allowed to hold real property; their limited rights, however, should be under "protection of the laws"); letter from William Heighton to George Stearns (Feb. 27, 1865), in *The Equality of Men before the Law Claimed and Defended in Speeches by William D. Kelley, Wendell Phillips and Frederick Douglass* (Boston, 1865).

Given the contractually based origin of the right to protection, one might logically assume that only citizens could claim this right. Such an assumption would, however, be incorrect. Relying on a concept of limited-implied allegiance, nineteenth-century authorities were unanimous in concluding that lawfully resident aliens also had a right to the protection of the sovereign authority. Only outlaws and slaves were denied this right. See, for example, *Clarke v. Morey*, 10 Johns 68 (N.Y. 1813); *Russel v. Skipwith*, 6 Binn. 241 (Pa. 1814); Kent, *Commentaries*, 1:62–63; Tucker, *Blackstone's Commentaries*, 2: app. 98.

ernment is called upon to resist a hostile invasion; with respect to citizens, mid-nineteenth-century thought also clearly posited a right to the protection of one's own government even while within the territorial jurisdiction of some other government.[19]

Another strand of the nineteenth-century concept of the right to protection derives from the somewhat ambiguous position of government itself. The central function of government is to protect fundamental rights. At the same time, however, government itself is potentially one of the greatest threats to these interests. For example, personal liberty is directly threatened by the power to imprison and the right to hold property by the powers of taxation and eminent domain.[20]

Kent dealt with this problem by describing a right to protection *from* government as well as *by* government.[21] In the landmark decision of *Ex Parte Milligan*, decided contemporaneously with the drafting of the Fourteenth Amendment, a majority of the justices of the Supreme Court relied heavily on this concept. Finding that a military tribunal had no jurisdiction to try and convict a civilian in a loyal state, Justice David Davis argued:

> [I]t is the birthright of every American citizen when charged with crime to be tried and punished according to law. The power of punishment is alone the means through which the laws have provided for the purpose and if they are ineffectual, there is an immunity from punishment.... By the protection of the law human rights are secured; withdraw that protection and they are at the mercy of wicked rulers, or the clamor of an excited people.[22]

---

19. See, for example, *Congressional Globe*, 39th Cong., 1st sess., 1090 (1866) (remarks of Rep. Bingham); 10 *Opinions of the Attorney General* 382, 404 (1862).

20. Calhoun, *Disquisition*, passim.

21. Kent, *Commentaries*, 1:331–332, 339.

22. *Ex Parte Milligan*, 71 U.S. (4 Wall.) 295 (1866). In addition, see 10 *Opinions of the Attorney General* 382, 393–394 (1862).

Milligan viewed the right to protection from government primarily in a procedural context. Kent, however, also described the right to protection from government as including a substantive component that shielded the citizenry from "unequal and undue assessments" and guaranteed compensation for the taking of property seized for public use.[23] In this context, issues of taxation were particularly prominent in the antebellum courts.

Prohibitions against unequal and unjust assessments were often embodied in state constitutional provisions requiring "uniformity" in taxation.[24] However, even where such clauses did not exist or were plainly inapplicable to the particular case at bar, courts often relied on the right to protection in striking down taxes that were patently unfair. The judicial response to laws allowing cities to tax property beyond their boundaries provides a classic example. In *Wells v. City of Weston*, the Missouri Supreme Court observed that no specific constitutional provision barred the practice. Nonetheless the court found the tax invalid, arguing:

> As the very purpose of instituting government is the protection of the citizen in his person and property, power to violate these rights would seem to be quite beyond the lawful authority of any government; and certainly the legislative department of this government can not arbitrarily take the property of one citizen and give it to another, and, of course can not authorize others to do so.... This... seems to be substantially the authority here given: those who live in the town are authorized to exact annually from those who live adjacent to it, a certain portion of their property, to be applied... to their own local purposes. And this we think can not be done under our govern-

23. Kent, *Commentaries*, 1:331–332, 339.

24. See, for example, Indiana Constitution of 1851, art. 10, sec. 1, reprinted in Swindler, *Sources and Documents*, 3:388; Minnesota Constitution of 1857, art. 9, sec. 1, reprinted in ibid., 5:311.

> ment, which was instituted exclusively for the protection of individual rights, and where private property is expressly protected from any appropriation of it... without full compensation to the owner.[25]

The supreme courts of Iowa and Kentucky struck down similar laws, noting that governmental protection was the quid pro quo that a citizen received for his taxes.[26] Thus, one who was taxed without receiving such protection was having his property seized for public use without compensation.

Another major theme of the tax cases was that the burden of taxation should be fairly distributed among those who would benefit from government programs. Most commonly, this theory was used to attack otherwise general property taxes that were qualified by the deliberate exclusion or underassessment of particular classes of property. The same concept, however, also forbade the imposition of unduly heavy burdens on a small class of taxpayers. The governing principle, as summarized by the Pennsylvania Supreme Court, was that "[t]he whole of a public burden cannot be thrown on a single individual, under pretence of taxing him, nor can one county be taxed to pay the debt of another, nor one portion of the state to pay the debts of the whole state."[27]

In short, in antebellum jurisprudence, the right to the protection of the law embraced a variety of interests. In general, the right described an absolute obligation of the government to every citizen. At the same time, the right was closely circumscribed by two factors. The first was the sharp distinction that was drawn between the right to protection and the right to benefits. Even

---

25. 22 Mo. 384, 388 (1856).

26. *Morford v. Unger*, 8 Iowa 82, 92–95 (1859); *City of Covington v. Southgate*, 54 Ky. 491 (1854). In addition, see Cooley, *Constitutional Limitations*, p. 495.

27. See, for example, *Sanborn v. Commissioners of Rice County*, 9 Minn. 273, 277 (1864); Cooley, *Constitutional Limitations*, p. 594; *Sharpless v. Mayor of Philadelphia*, 21 Penn. St. 147, 168 (1853).

those who advocated equality with respect to both made clear distinctions between the two concepts. For example, in vetoing the bill extending the life of the Second Bank of the United States, Andrew Jackson argued:

> Distinctions in society will always exist under every just government. Equality of talents, of education, or of wealth can not be produced by human institutions. In the full enjoyment of the gifts of Heaven and the fruits of superior industry, economy, and virtue, every man is equally entitled to protection by law; but when the laws undertake to add to these natural and just advantages artificial distinctions, to grant titles, gratuities, and exclusive privileges, to make the rich richer and the potent more powerful, the humble members of society—the farmers, mechanics, and laborers—who have neither the time nor the means of securing like favors to themselves, have a right to complain of the injustice of their Government. There are no necessary evils in government. Its evils exist only in its abuses. If it would confine itself to equal protection, and, as Heaven does its rains, shower its favors alike on the high and the low, the rich and the poor, it would be an unqualified blessing.... Many of our rich men have not been content with equal protection and equal benefits, but have besought us to make them richer by act of Congress.[28]

In part, of course, this passage embodies the general Jacksonian concern for equality. In addition, however, it reflects a clear di-

---

28. James D. Richardson, *A Compilation of the Messages and Papers of the Presidents*, vol. 2 (New York, 1896), 576, 590. In addition, see Ohio Constitution of 1851, art. 1, sec. 2, reprinted in Swindler, *Sources and Documents*, 7:558; Iowa Constitution of 1846, art. 1, sec. 2, reprinted in ibid., 3:434; L. B. Slamm, "The Tariff No. 1: Its Injustice on Principles of Revenue" (pamphlet) (New York, 1843), quoted in Richard Welter, *The Mind of America, 1820–1860* (New York, 1975), p. 75.

chotomy between the right to benefits and the right to protection of the laws. Whatever benefits governments choose to bestow should, of course, be distributed without favoritism. Nonetheless, the primary function of government is protection, which must be equally available to all.

The scope of the right to protection of the laws was also limited by its generally parasitic nature. One did not have a right to challenge the existing structure of legal rights under this rubric; instead, the right simply guaranteed access to the protective structures already in place. Thus, unless one could identify another interest established by either natural or positive law, invocation of the right to protection of the laws was virtually useless.

These principles strongly influenced the decision in *Roberts v. City of Boston.*[29] *Roberts* was an 1849 challenge to the maintenance of segregated schools in Boston. Arguing for the plaintiff, Charles Sumner relied in part on the provision of the Massachusetts Constitution that provided, "[A]ll men are born free and equal and have certain natural, essential, and inalienable rights, among which may be reckoned the right of enjoying and defending their lives and liberties." This provision, Sumner contended, established the proposition that whites and blacks were "equal before the law"; and since in his view, segregated schools were by their nature unequal, the maintenance of separate schools violated the state constitution.[30]

Speaking for the Court, Chief Justice Lemuel Shaw accepted the argument that the state constitutional provision established equality before the law. Nonetheless, Shaw rejected Sumner's ultimate conclusion, arguing:

> The great principle . . . is that by the constitution and laws of Massachusetts all persons . . . are equal before the law. This, as a broad general principle . . . is per-

---

29. 59 Mass. (5 Cush.) 198 (1849).
30. Sumner, *His Complete Works* (Boston, 1870–1883), 3:55–56, 70–81.

> fectly sound.... But when this great principle comes to be applied to the actual and various conditions of persons in society, it will not warrant the assertion, that men and women are legally clothed with the same civil and political powers, and that children and adults are legally to have the same functions and be subject to the same treatment; *but only that the rights of all, as they are settled and regulated by law, are equally entitled to the paternal consideration and protection of the law, for their maintenance and security*. What those rights are, to which individuals, in the infinite variety of circumstances by which they are surrounded in society, are entitled, must depend on laws adapted to their respective relations and conditions.[31]

The standard analysis of the *Roberts* case describes Sumner as a hero whose argument presaged the conceptions of racial equality later embodied in the Fourteenth Amendment, and Shaw as a villain whose retrograde views on the nature of equality were to haunt American jurisprudence for the next hundred years.[32] This characterization is problematic for at least two reasons. First, Shaw was not attempting to define the concept of equal protection of the laws; he was merely referring to the concept as a reference point to give content to the notion that all men are equal before the law. Second, and even more important, the structure of Shaw's opinion simply reflects the dichotomy between the concepts of equality of rights and equality of protection, respectively, that pervaded antebellum legal arguments generally. Those arguments were based on the premise that all men—black or white—are equally entitled to protection of the laws to enforce their legal rights; but unless a particular interest could be classi-

---

31. 59 Mass. at 206 (emphasis added).

32. Judith Baer, *Equality under the Constitution: Reclaiming the Fourteenth Amendment* (Ithaca, N.Y., 1983), p. 77; Hyman and Wiecek, *Equal Justice Under Law*, pp. 95–96; Leonard Levy, *The Law of the Commonwealth and Chief Justice Shaw* (Cambridge, Mass., 1957), pp. 108–117.

fied as a natural right, the legislature could withhold that interest from any class at will. Since public education was not viewed as a natural right, the right to equal protection would not have been violated even if blacks had been totally excluded.

Another important feature of antebellum thought was the close relationship between the right to protection and the right to due process of law. Analytically, the two concepts are mirror images. Each envisions the same core set of interests; while the right to protection focuses on the obligation of government to *preserve* those interests from outside interference, due process analysis describes the limitations on the authority of government to act positively to *deprive* people of those rights. At times, however, the boundaries between the two concepts become blurred.

The clearest example of the merger between the rights to protection and due process is Kent's concept of the right to protection from government; essentially, the parameters of that right were defined by the elements of due process of law. Even where protection *by* government is involved, however, some issues could be reconceptualized as due process problems. Consider, for example, a statute that deprives a particular class of the right to enforce contracts in court. On its face, the problem might seem to be that the disadvantaged class is being denied legal protection for its economic interests. But one might also argue that the affected class is being deprived of its right to contract—a due process concept. Either mode of analysis could serve as the basis for an attack on the statute. Given this situation, it is not surprising that nineteenth-century analysts at times seemed to view the right to protection of the laws and the right to due process as interchangeable.[33]

Nonetheless, the right to protection of the laws had an independent significance in the antislavery argument. In essence, abolitionists argued that the fundamental difficulty with slavery was that African American slaves were being *denied* the protection of

---

33. See, for example, Cooley, *Constitutional Limitations*, pp. 351–413; *Debates in Maryland Constitutional Convention of 1851*, pp. 195–196, 259–260.

law. From the antislavery perspective, the necessary protection for blacks had three components. First, the law should formally provide that the life, liberty, and property of African Americans would be protected. Second, African Americans should have access to the courts to gain redress for violation of these protective laws. Third, the government should provide actual physical protection for African Americans and their fundamental rights. Henry Stanton's 1837 argument against the maintenance of slavery in the District of Columbia is particularly evocative:

> Having robbed the slave of himself, and thus made him a thing, Congress is consistent in denying to him all of the protection of the law as a man. His labor is coerced by laws of Congress; no bargain is made, no wage is given. His provender and covering are at the will of the owner. His domestic and social rights are as entirely disregarded in the eye of the law as if the Deity had never instituted the enduring relations of husband and wife, parent and child, brother and sister.
>
> There is not the shadow of legal protection or the family state among the slaves of the district... neither is there any real protection for the lives and limbs of the slaves.... No slave can be a party before a judicial tribunal... in any species of action against any person, no matter how atrocious may have been the injury received. He is not known to the law as a person: much less, a person having civil rights....
>
> To give impartial legal protection in [the] District to all of its inhabitants would annihilate slavery. Give the slave then, equal legal protection with his master, and at its first approach slavery and the slavery trade flee in panic as the darkness before the full-orbed sun.[34]

---

34. "Remarks by Henry Stanton before the Massachusetts House of Representatives," reprinted in E. Bormann, *Forerunners of Black Power: The Rhetoric of*

Opponents of slavery also invoked the right to protection in other, narrower contexts. For example, this concept played an important role in the antislavery argument against the Fugitive Slave Acts. In the free states, blacks were presumed to be free men unless proven otherwise. Thus, they would have as much right to the protection of the law as those asserting a constitutional right to reclaim escaped slaves. Antislavery theorists argued that by allowing the claimant to prevail simply on a claim that service was due, the Act unconstitutionally deprived the putative slave of equal protection.[35]

Further, although the Comity Clause was generally featured more prominently, the right to protection was also at times used by antebellum Republicans to criticize restrictions on free blacks. The 1858 debate over the admission of Oregon to the Union provides a particularly striking example. The proposed state constitution of Oregon not only outlawed slavery, but it also prohibited the immigration of free blacks into the state. Further, the constitution barred all blacks from access to the state courts. Most of the race-related criticism of the proposed constitution focused on the claim that the immigration restriction violated the Comity Clause. However, some Republicans also argued that even if the immigration restriction were acceptable, the ban on court access would be objectionable on the independent ground that it effectively denied the protection of law to blacks who might legitimately be in Oregon on temporary business.[36]

Abolition (Englewood Cliffs, N.J., 1971), pp. 63–64. In addition, see William Goodell, *American Slave Code* (1853, reprinted New York, 1969), pp. 23–44; Charles Olcott, *Two Lectures on the Subject of Slavery and Abolition* (Ohio, 1838); *Philanthropist*, Jan. 27, 1837, at 2 col. 2; Howard Jay Graham, *Everyman's Constitution: Historical Essays on the Fourteenth Amendment, the "Conspiracy Theory," and American Constitutionalism* (Madison, Wis., 1947), pp. 152–241; tenBroek, *Antislavery Origins.*

35. *In re Booth*, 3 Wis. 13, 44–45 (1854); Salmon P. Chase, *Argument in the Case of Wharton Jones v. John Van Zandt* (Cincinnati, 1847), p. 74.

36. *Congressional Globe*, 35th Cong., 1st sess., 1967 (1858) (remarks of Sen. Wilson); *Oregon Constitutional Debates of 1857*, p. 358.

The right to protection from government also found its way into other Republican arguments supporting the interests of free blacks. A prime example is the 1860 debate over education in the District of Columbia. As initially proposed, the bill before the Senate provided simply that the city authorities could impose a property tax to benefit the public schools in the District, and that the federal government would provide matching funds of up to $25,000 per year. Senate Republicans pressed for an amendment that would require the city government to use at least part of the funds to educate blacks as well as whites. One of the mainstays of the Republican argument was the contention that "taxing [blacks] for the exclusive benefit of the white children... would be a kind of legal robbery"[37]—a clear reference to the principles of the state taxation cases. Indeed, Republican Daniel Clark—the sponsor of the amendment to require that blacks be admitted to the schools—stated that he would accept a prohibition of blacks so long as they were exempted from the property tax and their pro rata share of the federal contribution was withheld.[38]

The connection between the concept of equal protection and the evolution of antislavery constitutional theory should not surprise those familiar with the role that the Equal Protection Clause has played in the development of modern constitutional law. However, the same concepts were at least equally important in the construction of the justifications for the proslavery position. The relationship between the right to protection of the law and proslavery theory was quite complex. On one hand, proslavery theorists were compelled to respond to antislavery arguments that relied on the right to protection of the law. On the other, the same right was of critical importance to the proslavery argument on slavery in the territories.

Proslavery legal theorists had some difficulty with the claim that slaves were entitled to the protection of the law. One posi-

---

37. *Congressional Globe*, 36th Cong., 1st sess., 1681 (1860).
38. Ibid., p. 1680.

tion was simply that slaves had no such right. This position was adopted by the South Carolina Supreme Court in *State v. Harden*, where the opinion stated flatly: "Slaves are chattels and their right of protection belongs to the master and is, therefore, not cast, as far as regards them personally, on society."[39] The majority view, however, was that "the law... recognizes [the slave's] existence as a person [and therefore] within the law's protecting powers"[40]—a principle that was generally embodied in statutes protecting slaves' lives and bodily integrity.

With respect to free blacks, the theoretical framework of slave-state courts was almost identical to that which underlay Chief Justice Shaw's opinion in the *Roberts* case. African Americans were not granted the same legal rights as whites; however, with respect to those rights which free blacks did possess, they were equally entitled to the protection of the law. In this context, the statement of the *Harden* Court is typical:

> Free Negroes, without any of the political rights which belong to a citizen, are still, to some extent, regarded by the law as possessing both natural and civil rights. The rights of life, liberty and property, belong to them, and must be protected by the community in which they are suffered to live. They are regarded, in law, as persons capable of committing and receiving an injury; and for the one, they are liable to punishment, for the other, they are entitled to redress.[41]

---

39. 29 S.C.L. (2 Speers) 152, 154 (1832). In addition, see *State v. Mann*, 13 N.C. (2 Dev.) 263 (1829); *Ex Parte Boylston*, 33 S.C.L. (2 Strob.) 41, 43 (1847).

40. Thomas R. R. Cobb, *An Inquiry into the Law of Negro Slavery in the United States* (n.p., 1858, reprinted New York, 1968), 2:82–96. In addition, see *Fields v. State*, 9 Tenn. (1 Yer.) 156 (1829); *State v. Reed*, 9 N.C. (2 Hawks.) 454 (1823).

41. 29 S.C.L. (2 Speers) 152, 154 (1832). In addition, see *State v. Manuel*, 20 N.C. (4 Dev. and Bat. Eq.) 77 (1838); *Ely v. Thompson*, 10 Ky. (3 A.K. Marsh) 981 (1820).

Despite such pronouncements, the attitude of Southern whites toward blacks put considerable pressure on the idea that blacks possessed fully the right to protection. The issue came to a head in the Maryland Constitutional Convention of 1851. An attempt was made to amend the state bill of rights so that the due process clause would apply only to citizens, rather than to all free men. The avowed purpose of the sponsors of the proposal was to allow the state legislature to banish all free blacks from the state. Opponents argued that the change would in essence place blacks outside the protection of the law; proponents responded that free blacks would still be protected from murder, kidnapping, and the like.[42] Ultimately the convention left the basic due process clause unchanged, but added a provision that stated,"[N]othing in this article shall be so construed, as to prevent the legislature from passing all such laws for the government, regulation and disposition of the free colored population in this state as they see fit."[43]

The dynamic of the Maryland Convention was in many ways typical of the antebellum debates over the rights of free blacks generally. Even defenders of slavery did not wish to be viewed as taking actions inconsistent with the fundamental rights of free blacks as human beings. At the same time, however, the general distaste for blacks generated pressure for oppressive measures that would be viewed as intolerable if applied to whites. Thus, while giving lip service to the concept that blacks were equally entitled to the "protection of the law," both slave and free states adopted policies that made clear their view that for blacks, the right to protection was severely limited.[44] This trend accelerated in the decade prior to the Civil War, with slave-state governments in particular taking actions that increasingly limited the fundamental rights of free blacks within their jurisdiction.

---

42. *Debates in Maryland Constitutional Convention of 1851*, pp. 195–196, 259–260.

43. Ibid., p. 196.

44. *State v. Manuel*, 20 N.C. (4 Dev. and Bat. Eq.) 177 (1838); *State v. Harden*, 29 S.C.L. (2 Speers) 152 (1832).

The concept of equal protection was also central to the antebellum defense of slavery itself. Slaveowners argued that slaves were a constitutionally recognized species of property and, as such, were entitled to be equally protected with other types of property. This point was central to Chief Justice Roger Brooke Taney's argument in *Prigg v. Pennsylvania*. In *Prigg*, Justice Joseph Story spoke for the majority in concluding that states were prohibited from adopting statutes in aid of slaveowners' constitutionally protected rights to recover fugitives. Dissenting, Taney relied on the concept of equal protection in contending that states were in fact *required* to provide aid to the slaveowners.

> The words of the article [of the Constitution] which direct that the fugitive "shall be delivered up" seem evidently designed to impose it as a duty upon the people of the several States to pass laws to carry into execution, in good faith, the compact into which they thus solemnly entered with each other...why may not a State protect a right of property acknowledged by its own term outlaw? Besides, the laws of the different States in all other cases, constantly protect the citizens of other states in their rights of property when it is bound within their respective territories...in the absence of any express prohibition, I perceive no reason for establishing by implication, a different rule in this instance, where, by the national compact, this right of property is recognized as an existing right in every State of the Union.[45]

More commonly, the concept of equal protection was invoked in support of the argument that slavery should be allowed in the territories. The proslavery forces recognized that it was not enough to prevent the taking of their property through the use of the Due Process Clause. Because of the nature of slave property, slavery required positive action by government to enforce the slave-

45. 41 U.S. (16 Pet.) at 620 (1842).

holder's ability to hold persons in bondage and coerce labor from them, as well as to regulate the relationship between master and slave generally. Thus, many proslavery theorists did not simply argue that Congress was constitutionally required to tolerate slavery in the territories. They also contended that, since slaveholders had the right to protection of the law for their property, Congress had to provide at least some mechanism by which such protection could be obtained.[46]

Initially, most proslavery theorists did not demand that territorial laws contain special provisions governing slaveholder's rights. Instead, they were willing to leave the protection of slave property in the hands of the common-law courts, despite the fact that such a policy would often render the maintenance of slavery untenable. This approach fit comfortably with the basic Southern theory regarding slavery in the territories. Under that theory, Congress had authority neither to prohibit nor to establish slavery in the territories, and passage of a slave code might be construed as the establishment of slavery. By contrast, mere reliance on the courts would simply be an appeal to the generally accepted obligation of government to provide protection for property rights established by another source of law.[47]

Despite its theoretical attractiveness, the policy of "nonintervention" that this theory espoused lost support in the Southern states in the late 1850s. The potential difficulties deriving from the lack of a slave code were apparent from the beginning; moreover, Southern radicals argued that the experience in Kansas

---

46. *Congressional Globe*, 31st Cong., 1st sess., 1003, app. 917 (1850) (remarks of Sen. Davis); "Platform of Alabama State Democratic Convention of 1848," in *Louisville Daily Courier*, Feb. 22, 1860, quoted in Dwight L. Dumond, ed., *Southern Editorials on Secession* (Gloucester, Mass., 1964), p. 39.

47. *Congressional Globe*, 34th Cong., 3d sess., 103–104 (1856) (remarks of Rep. Orr); ibid., p. 67 (remarks of Rep. Smith); "Address of the Southern Delegates in Congress to their Constituents," in Richard K. Cralle, ed., *The Works of John C. Calhoun* (New York, 1851–57), 6:290–313; Don E. Fehrenbacher, *The Dred Scott Case: Its Significance in American Law and Politics* (New York, 1978), ch. 6.

demonstrated the inadequacy of nonintervention theory in practice. The complaint of the *Charleston Mercury* is typical:

> Has the principle of equal protection to slave property been carried out by the Government [in Kansas] in any of its departments?...while impunity and license was given to abolition roughians and Northern disturbers of the public peace of the John Brown school, the army of the United States was used to check the vindication of Southern Rights unprotected by the Government. Have not the officers of justice, time and again, quashed indictments against the perturbers of the security of Southern men and Southern property—murders, incendiaries, and Negro thieves, etc.?...in our opinion, had the principle of equal protection to Southern men and Southern property been rigorously observed by the General Government, both California and Kansas would undoubtedly have come into the Union as Slave States. The South lost those states for the lack of proper assertion of this great principle.[48]

Seemingly vindicated in their constitutional theories by Taney's opinion in *Dred Scott*, Southerners pressed for a territorial slave code to remedy what they perceived as the denial of their right to the equal protection of the laws. On February 2, 1860, Jefferson Davis introduced a set of resolutions in the Senate that denied congressional power "to annul or impair the constitutional right of any citizen of the United States to take his slave property into the common Territories, and there hold and enjoy the same while the territorial condition remains" and established a congressional duty to act to remedy any deficiency in "means to

---

48. Dumond, *Southern Editorials*, pp. 42–43. In addition, see *Richmond Enquirer*, May 8, 1960, in ibid., pp. 78–83; *Augusta Daily Chronicle and Sentinel*, May 24, 1860, in ibid., p. 111; Fehrenbacher, *The Dred Scott Case*, chs. 20–21.

insure adequate protection to constitutional right in a territory." The more radical Albert Gallatin Brown introduced a resolution calling even more explicitly for the enactment of territorial slave codes. At the Democratic convention in Charleston, the proslavery forces proposed similar language for the party platform; when the supporters of Senator Stephen A. Douglas refused to acquiesce in this language, Southern Democrats chose to form their own party, splitting the national Democracy and ultimately assuring the election of Lincoln. Finally, in the deliberations of the Committee of Thirteen, formed in a last-ditch effort to preserve the Union without war, Robert Toombs of Georgia proposed constitutional amendments that would have provided "[t]hat the people of the United States shall have an equal right to emigrate to and settle in the present or any future acquired territories, with whatever property they may possess, (including slaves), and be securely protected in its peaceful enjoyment" and "[t]hat property in slaves shall be entitled to the same protection from the government of the United States in all its departments everywhere which the constitution confers the power upon it to extend to any property."[49]

Obviously, Toombs's proposal never became a part of the Constitution. Instead, eight years later, section 1 of the Fourteenth Amendment would include an equal protection provision that would become the bulwark of the rights of the slaves freed after the Civil War. However, those who drafted the Fourteenth Amendment did not view the Equal Protection Clause as the centerpiece of section 1. Rather, they believed that the Privileges and Immunities Clause provided far more significant protection for the rights of free blacks. Like the Equal Protection Clause, the

---

49. *Congressional Globe*, 36th Cong., 1st sess., 658, 935 (1860); ibid., p. 1001; *Charleston Mercury*, May 3, 1860, in Dumond, *Southern Editorials*, pp. 71–73; *Richmond Enquirer*, May 8, 1860, in ibid., pp. 77–83; *Augusta Daily Chronicle and Sentinel*, May 24, 1860, in ibid., pp. 108–112; Dwight L. Dumond, *The Secession Movement, 1860–1861* (New York, 1931), chs. 3–5; Sen. Rep. 288, 36th Cong., 2d sess., at 2–3 (1860).

language of the Privileges and Immunities Clause had deep roots in pre-Civil War legal thought.

Privileges and Immunities

The concept of the privileges and immunities of citizenship played a prominent role in both state and federal constitutions in the antebellum era. At the state level, the Indiana, Iowa, and Oregon constitutions provided that the legislature "shall not grant to any citizen, or class of citizens, privileges or immunities which, upon the same terms, shall not belong equally to all citizens."[50] The Ohio Constitution provided that any grant of such privileges or immunities should be subject to legislative revocation.[51] Other states adopted related provisions.[52] In this context, however, the state constitutions were not the direct precursors of section 1 of the Fourteenth Amendment. Instead, the Fourteenth Amendment language can be traced to Article IV, section 2 of the original Constitution—the Comity Clause—which provides that "[t]he Citizens of each state shall be entitled to all Privileges and Immunities of Citizens in the several States." Despite the near-identity in language, the Comity Clause performed a function quite different from the facially similar state provisions.

At the state level, the privileges and immunities provisions were aimed at "class legislation"—but not the same species of class legislation that was generally subjected to due process attack. Rather than guaranteeing that discrete classes of individuals

---

50. Indiana Constitution of 1851, art. 1, sec. 23, reprinted in Swindler, *Sources and Documents*, 3:379; Iowa Constitution of 1846, art. 1, sec. 6, reprinted in ibid., 3:435; Oregon Constitution of 1857, art. 1, sec. 21, reprinted inibid., 8:206.

51. Ohio Constitution of 1851, art. 1, sec. 2, reprinted in ibid., 7:558.

52. For example, see Texas Constitution of 1845, art. 1, sec. 2, reprinted in ibid., 9:260; Virginia Constitution of 1776, Bill of Rights, sec. 3, reprinted in ibid., 7:49.

would not be *denied* natural or vested rights, these provisions prevented legislatures from *granting* additional, special rights to individuals. For example, in *McRee v. Wilmington & R.R. Co.*,[53] the North Carolina Supreme Court held that the state privileges and immunities clause barred the grant of a monopoly right to operate a bridge across a particular river. Similarly, in *Norwich Gaslight Co. v. Norwich City Gas Co.*,[54] the Connecticut Supreme Court struck down a government-imposed gas monopoly on the same grounds. Monopoly charters for roads and ferries were also prominently mentioned in discussions of state privileges and immunities clauses.[55]

The Comity Clause, by contrast, performs a quite different function. All agreed that this clause guaranteed every citizen the right to travel freely throughout the country without interference by the various state governments. Moreover, with respect to other rights, the almost universal opinion was that the clause did not affect the relationship between a state and its own citizens. Instead, the Comity Clause was held to constrain only the actions of state governments with respect to citizens of other states. The dominant approach to interpretation of this clause adopted the position that it was only intended to prevent *discrimination* by one state against residents of other states. Joseph Story put the point succinctly:

> [I]t is obvious, that, if the citizens of each state were to be deemed aliens to each other they could not take, or hold real estate, or other privileges, except as other aliens. The intention of [the Comity Clause] was to confer on them, . . . a general citizenship; and to communicate all the privileges and immunities, which the

53. 47 N.C. 186 (1855).
54. 25 Conn. 19 (1856).
55. See *Debates and Proceedings, Indiana Constitutional Convention of 1850–1851*, pp. 385, 1391–1430.

> citizens of the same state would be entitled to under the like circumstances.[56]

Chancellor Kent took precisely the same view. In *Livingston v. Van Ingen*, he asserted that "[the Comity Clause] means only that citizens of other states shall have equal rights with our own citizens, and not that they shall have different or greater rights."[57] Kent reaffirmed this position in his *Commentaries*, noting that "if [citizens] remove from one state to another, they are entitled to the privileges that persons of the same description are entitled to in the state to which the removal is made, and to none other."[58]

Prior to the Civil War, the Supreme Court implicitly endorsed the Story/Kent approach in *Conner v. Elliott*. There the Court faced a dispute over the disposition of certain Louisiana property whose owner had died. One of the claimants was the owner's widow, a citizen of Mississippi. Under Louisiana law, if the marriage had been contracted in Louisiana, the widow could have claimed the property. By contrast, property rights derived from out-of-state marriages were to be governed by the law of the state in which the marriage was contracted or (under certain circumstances) the marital domicile. The widow claimed that this discrimination violated the Comity Clause. The Court, however, unanimously rejected this argument, concluding that "[t]he statute does not discriminate between citizens of the State and other persons; it discriminates between contracts only. Such discrimination has no connection with [the Comity Clause]."[59]

Contemporaneously with the ratification of the Fourteenth Amendment, the Court reaffirmed this view in *Paul v. Virginia*.[60] Speaking for a unanimous Court, Justice Stephen Field asserted:

---

56. Joseph Story, *Commentaries on the Constitutions of the United States* (Boston, 1833), pp. 674–675.
57. 9 Johns 509, 576 (1812).
58. Kent, *Commentaries*, 2:71.
59. 60 U.S. (18 How.) 591, 594 (1856).
60. 75 U.S. (8 Wall.) 168 (1868).

> It was undoubtedly the object of [the Comity Clause] to place the citizens of each State *upon the same footing* with citizens of other States, as far as the advantages resulting from citizenship in those States are concerned. It relieves them from the disabilities of alienage in other States; it gives them the right of free ingress into other States, and free egress from them; it insures to them in other States the same freedom possessed by the citizens of those States in the acquisition of property and in the pursuit of happiness; and it secures to them in other States the equal protection of the laws.[61]

In short, the prevailing view of the Comity Clause in the early nineteenth century was that it was simply an antidiscrimination provision. The reach of the clause was limited in other ways as well. Most courts concluded that the concept of "privileges and immunities" did not encompass all rights that were associated with citizenship in a particular state; rather, only those rights that were in some sense "fundamental" were viewed as protected. The opinion of the Maryland Supreme Court in *Campbell v. Morris* is typical:

> It seems agreed, from the manner of expounding, or defining the words immunities and privileges, by the counsel on both sides that a particular and limited operation is to be given to these words, and not a full and comprehensive one. It is agreed it does not mean the right of election, the right of holding offices, the right of being elected. The Court are of the opinion that it means that the citizens of all the States shall have the peculiar advantage of acquiring and holding real as well as personal property, and that such property shall be protected and secured by the laws of the State, in the same manner as the property of the citi-

61. Ibid., p. 180 (emphasis added).

> zens of the State is protected. It means, such property shall not be liable to any taxes, or burdens which the property of the citizens is not subject to.
>
> It may also mean, that, as creditors, they shall be on the same footing with the State creditor, in the payment of the debts of a deceased debtor.[62]

The *Connor/Campbell* view of the Comity Clause fit comfortably into the state-centered structure of the antebellum era. States were seen as the primary definers of rights; the function of federal law was to ensure that those rights were not defined in a way that was inconsistent with the concept of a national union. The nondiscrimination approach to Comity Clause analysis was consistent with both elements of this model. Nonetheless, some antebellum authorities took a different view, embracing an absolute rights theory of privileges and immunities. The absolute rights theory conceded that the clause only protected citizens from outside the relevant state; however, the theory posited a core set of rights belonging to citizens independent of the laws of that state. It was these rights that the Comity Clause was said to protect.[63]

This view, however, had little support in the case law. Admittedly, many nineteenth-century jurists posited the existence of a core set of fundamental rights. Nonetheless, few Comity Clause decisions suggested that Article IV provided a guarantee of these rights if they were denied by the positive law of the state in which a person was temporarily present.

Justice Bushrod Washington's widely-cited opinion in *Corfield v. Coryell* provides a somewhat equivocal exception. In that case, sitting on circuit, Justice Washington rejected a Comity Clause-based attack on a state law that forbade citizens from other states

---

62. 3 Harris and McHenry, 535, 554 (Md. 1797). In addition, see *Corfield v. Coryell*, 6 F. Cas. 546 (C.C.E.D. Pa. 1823) (no. 3230); *Abbot v. Bayley*, 23 Mass. (6 Pick.) 89, 92 (1827); Kettner, *The Development of American Citizenship*, ch. 9.

63. John Coleman Hurd, *The Law of Freedom and Bondage in the United States* (Boston, 1862), 2:660–670.

from dredging oysters. In the course of his opinion, Washington discussed the general scope of the Comity Clause:

> The inquiry is, what are the privileges and immunities of citizens in the several states? We feel no hesitation in confining these expressions to those privileges and immunities which are, in their nature, fundamental; which belong, of right, to the citizens of all free governments; and which have, at all times, been enjoyed by the citizens of the several states which compose this Union, from the time of their becoming free, independent, and sovereign. What these fundamental principles are, it would perhaps be more tedious than difficult to enumerate. They may, however, be all comprehended under the following general heads: Protection by the government; the enjoyment of life and liberty, with the right to acquire and possess property of every kind and to pursue and obtain happiness and safety; subject nevertheless to such restraints as the government may justly prescribe for the general good of the whole. The right of a citizen of one state to pass through, or to reside in any other state, for purposes of trade, agriculture, professional pursuits, or otherwise; to claim the benefit of the writ of habeas corpus; to institute and maintain actions of any kind in the courts of the state; to take, hold and dispose of property, either real or personal; and an exemption from higher taxes or impositions than are paid by the other citizens of the state may be mentioned as some of the particular privileges and immunities of citizens, which are clearly embraced by the general description of privileges deemed to be fundamental: to which may be added, the elective franchise, as regulated and established by the laws or constitution of the state in which it is to be exercised. These, and many others which might be mentioned, are, strictly speaking, privileges and immunities, and the

> enjoyment of them by the citizens of each state, in every other state, was manifestly calculated (to use the expressions of the preamble of the corresponding provision in the old articles of confederation) "the better to secure and perpetuate mutual friendship and intercourse among the people of the different states of the Union."[64]

Taken out of context, this language might seem to provide support for the absolute rights view of the Comity Clause. However, Washington was *not* seeking to expand the reach of the clause; instead, he was seeking to define the *limitations* of the privileges and immunities concept. Thus, as support for the absolute rights position, the *Corfield* opinion is ambiguous at best.

In any event, in most contexts the difference between the two theories was of little practical import. First, both theories held that the Comity Clause dealt only with the relationship between a state and citizens of a different state. Second, the antidiscrimination theorists limited the effect of the clause to the same fundamental rights upon which absolute rights theorists based their argument. Further, the idea of a state government failing to provide its own citizens generally with the rights discussed in *Corfield* was almost unthinkable; thus, those rights would be guaranteed to the citizens of other states even under the antidiscrimination theory. In most cases involving the rights of whites, then, both theories yielded essentially the same results. By contrast, in the struggle over the status of slavery and the rights of free blacks, the choice between Comity Clause theories at times became critical. Moreover, neither antislavery nor proslavery theorists showed a consistent preference for either the federalism/antidiscrimination view or the absolute rights position; instead, both sides shifted ground, depending on which approach to the Comity Clause was more advantageous to the argument that they were making.

Prior to the Civil War, those who sought to find protection for

64. 6 F. Cas. 546, 551–552 (C.C.E.D. Pa. 1823) (no. 3320).

free blacks in the Constitution often focused their attention on the Comity Clause. Arguing that free blacks were citizens of their home states, pro-black politicians generally focused on the federalism/antidiscrimination interpretation of the Privileges and Immunities Clause and argued that the blacks' rights as citizens should also be protected when they traveled to other states. These arguments were applied against free states as well as slave states. For example, in *Crandall v. State*, the Comity Clause was invoked in an inconclusive attack on a Connecticut law that prohibited the establishment of schools for the education of blacks who were not residents of that state.[65]

Some students of antislavery constitutionalism treat *Crandall* as a landmark case in which Crandall's counsel developed innovative legal arguments.[66] In fact, the use of the Comity Clause in the argument was a simple application of a well-established legal principle—that with respect to certain rights, the Constitution forbade states to discriminate against residents of other states. Further, the key issue in *Crandall*—whether free blacks were in fact citizens and thus within the protection of Article IV—was debated in a variety of contexts both prior to and contemporaneously with the *Crandall* controversy. Thus, to suggest that the case is a legal landmark substantially overstates its importance.[67]

The sectional conflict was more clearly implicated in other attempts to bring free blacks within the protection of the Comity Clause. One prominent issue was the dispute over the Negro Seamen's Acts. Beginning in 1822, South Carolina and other Southern states adopted statutes requiring that black crew members of any ship coming into port be arrested and held in jail until their vessel departed and that they be sold into slavery unless the cap-

---

65. *Crandall v. State*, 10 Conn. 339 (1834).

66. Dwight L. Dumond, *Antislavery: The Crusade for Freedom in America* (Ann Arbor, 1961), ch. 25; Graham, *Everyman's Constitution*, pp. 176–185.

67. William M. Wiecek, *The Sources of Anti-Slavery Constitutionalism in America, 1760–1848* (Ithaca, N.Y., 1977), pp. 163–167, appears to take a similar view of the significance of *Crandall*.

tain of their ship paid the expenses incurred by the state for their room and board. Northern states complained that the free blacks on board the vessels were citizens of those states. Therefore, they contended, to subject them to the Negro Seamen's Acts was inconsistent with the Comity Clause.[68]

While the Negro Seamen's Acts were a more or less constant source of friction in the antebellum era, the most significant invocation of the Comity Clause in this context came in the celebrated Samuel Hoar affair. Seeking to generate a dispositive judicial challenge to the statutes, the Massachusetts legislature sent Hoar to Charleston, South Carolina. Upon his arrival, resolutions passed by the South Carolina legislature denounced Hoar as "the emissary of a foreign Government" who must be expelled because of his seditious purposes. Further, the mood of the populace of Charleston itself made Hoar's personal safety uncertain. Thus, after consultation with leading citizens of the city, Hoar departed Charleston without accomplishing his mission.[69]

Many Northerners were greatly offended by the treatment that Hoar received. Antislavery politicians made repeated references to the incident in the 1850s and 1860s. Northern members of Congress continued to assert that the Negro Seamen's Act of South Carolina violated the Comity Clause by its own terms. Now, however, those claims were linked with complaints that the state had denied the protection of the clause to Hoar himself by effectively refusing him access to the state judicial system.[70]

Attacks on state laws prohibiting the immigration of free Ne-

---

68. H. R. Rep. 80, 27th Cong., 3d sess., 2 (1843); Fehrenbacher, *The Dred Scott Case*, pp. 69–71; Henry Wilson, *History of the Rise and Fall of the Slave Power in America* (Boston, 1872), 1:576–586; Carl B. Swisher, *History of the Supreme Court of the United States: The Taney Period: 1836–1864* (New York, 1974), 378–382, 392–393.

69. George F. Hoar, *Autobiography of Seventy Years* (New York, 1903), 1:24–27; Wilson, *Rise and Fall*, 1:578–582.

70. *Congressional Globe*, 39th Cong., 1st sess., 474 (1866); ibid., 33d Cong., 1st sess., app. 1012–1013 (1854); ibid., 31st Cong., 1st sess., app. 1661–1662 (1850) (remarks of Sen. Winthrop).

groes were also at times based on the Comity Clause. Some more radical antislavery legislators relied on this provision in the debates over the admission of Missouri to the Union in 1821 and the admission of Oregon in 1859. In both cases, the proposed state constitutions prohibited blacks from entering the state. In each case, numerous pro-black representatives explicitly made the presence of such a constitutional provision the basis for opposing admission. Similarly, Comity Clause arguments were a mainstay of opposition to attempts to add anti-immigration provisions to the constitutions of existing states.[71]

On this issue, however, the antislavery forces were not united. In the debates over Oregon, for example, Senator Lyman Trumbull of Illinois explicitly disavowed the constitutional attacks on the anti-immigration provision. Nonetheless, the Oregon debates are particularly important elements in the background of the development of the Fourteenth Amendment. During those debates, Representative John A. Bingham of Ohio explicitly embraced a theory of the Comity Clause that went beyond even the conventional absolute rights theory:

> The citizens of each state, all the citizens of each state, being citizens of the United States, shall be entitled to "all privileges and immunities of citizens in the several states." . . . [T]here is an ellipsis in the language employed in the constitution, but its meaning is self evident that it is "the privileges and immunities of citizens of the United States in the several states" that it guarantees.[72]

---

71. Ibid., 35th Cong., 2d sess., 982–985 (1859) (remarks of Rep. Bingham); ibid., 974–975 (remarks of Rep. Dawes); *Annals of Congress*, 16th Cong., 2d sess., 92–94 (1820) (remarks of Sen. Otis); Kettner, *Development of American Citizenship*, pp. 312–313; *Debates and Proceedings, Indiana Constitutional Convention of 1850–51*, pp. 438–462, 561–644; *Debates and Proceedings, Illinois Constitutional Convention of 1847*, pp. 201–228, 855–863.

72. *Congressional Globe*, 35th Cong., 1st sess., 1964–1965 (1858). In addition, see *Debates and Proceedings, Indiana Constitutional Convention of 1850–51*, pp. 572–576. *Congressional Globe*, 35th Cong., 2d sess., 984 (1859).

Bingham's invocation of the Comity Clause as a limitation on the ability of states to deal with their own citizenry was truly novel. Although some abolitionists had argued that the federal government had implicit authority to protect the "privileges and immunities" appurtenant to national citizenship, they had relied on other clauses as the source of the rights and concomitant power.[73] On its face, Bingham's argument might seem to have posed a substantial threat to the state-centered antebellum concept of federalism. However, two facets of Bingham's position sharply limited its potential in this regard.

First, like his contemporaries, Bingham plainly viewed the guarantees of the Comity Clause as applicable only to a narrow, fixed set of interests. He argued that under the Constitution,

> all... classes [of] free inhabitants, irrespective of ages, sex or complexion, and their descendants were [made] citizens of the United States. No distinctions were made against the poor and in favor of the rich and against the free-born blacks and in favor of the whites. This Government rests upon the absolute equality of natural rights among men. There is *not*, and cannot be, *any equality in the enjoyment of political or conventional rights.*[74]

The import of this argument is clear; Bingham viewed the Comity Clause as relevant only to issues of natural rights and those rights necessarily inherent in citizenship.

Even more importantly, while Bingham posited the existence of constitutionally guaranteed universal rights, he denied that Congress had general authority to enforce those rights. This position followed logically from the theory of the Fugitive Slave

---

73. Lysander Spooner, *The Unconstitutionality of Slavery* (Boston, 1845), ch. 8; Joel Tiffany, *A Treatise on the Unconstitutionality of Slavery* (Cleveland, 1849), chs. 12–16; tenBroek, *Equal under Law*, pp. 108–112.

74. *Congressional Globe*, 35th Cong., 2d sess., 985 (1859) (emphasis added).

Clause developed by Salmon P. Chase. Chase contended that because the Constitution granted no explicit authority to Congress to enforce that clause, no such authority could be inferred. Because both the Fugitive Slave Clause and the Comity Clause are contained in Article IV, section 2, the argument necessarily implies that Congress also lacked authority to enforce the guarantee of privileges and immunities—a point Bingham would later emphasize when he introduced an early draft of section 1 of the Fourteenth Amendment.[75] Thus, taken as a whole, Bingham's theory posed no real threat to state autonomy in the antebellum era. In slightly altered form, however, it was to reemerge in the Reconstruction era as one of the mainstays of the theory supporting national intervention to protect civil rights.

The concept of privileges and immunities of national citizenship also figured prominently in the proslavery argument. The Southern approach to the Comity Clause had both a defensive and an offensive component. First, Southerners were forced to deal with antislavery claims that various actions taken by the slave states were unconstitutional under the Privileges and Immunities Clause. Second, they sought to invoke the Comity Clause to force recognition of slaveholders' rights in certain circumstances.

Of necessity, the proslavery response to antislavery Comity Clause arguments was multifaceted. With respect to claims that specific whites such as Samuel Hoar had been mistreated, the Southern response was simply that the facts had been misreported.[76] In order to adequately defend both general prohibitions on black immigration and measures such as the Negro Seamen's Act, however, a more sophisticated theoretical framework was required.

---

75. Ibid., 31st Cong., 1st sess., app. 476–477 (1850). In addition, see *In re Booth*, 3 Wis. 13, 51 (1854); Sumner, "Freedom National Slavery Sectional," in Sumner, *His Complete* Works, 2:257–366, pp. 322–324; *Congressional Globe*, 39th Cong., 1st sess., 157–158, 1064, 1292 (1866).

76. Ibid., 33d Cong., 1st sess., 1556 (1854); ibid., 31st Cong., 1st sess., app. 288–289 (1850).

The basic Southern defense of these provisions rested on the contention that blacks were not citizens within the meaning of Article IV, and thus were not entitled to the protection of the Comity Clause. On this point Southern theorists relied on two analytically distinct arguments. Some used a state-centered view of national citizenship. They contended that national citizenship was derivative of state citizenship, and that even free blacks generally lacked many of the rights normally associated with citizenship in their home states and would not be considered citizens in those states.[77] Other Southern theorists took a different view, asserting that citizenship for purposes of the Comity Clause was defined by national standards that excluded blacks. In *Mitchell v. Wells*, Judge William L. Harris of Mississippi cast this argument in bluntly racist terms, conceding that Northern states, if they wished, might "confer citizenship on the chimpanzee or ourange-outange [sic]," but arguing that such a decision would not "require of the States not thus demented, to forget their own policy... and lower their own citizens... to meet the necessities of the mongrel race thus attempted to be introduced into the family of sisters in this confederacy."[78]

Neither approach was free from difficulty. First, any rights-focused conception of citizenship required the definition of a core set of rights that constituted the sine qua non of citizenship. Admittedly, many Northern states denied a wide variety of rights to their free black inhabitants—particularly purely political rights. However, those same rights were generally denied to groups such as women and children, whom all conceded had the status of citizens under the Constitution. Indeed, in the early nineteenth century, the most widely held view was that all free inhabitants who owed allegiance to a particular sovereign were citizens of that

---

77. See, for example, *Amy v. Smith*, 1 Littell 326 (Ky. 1822); 1 *Opinions of the Attorney General* 506 (1821).

78. 37 Miss. 235, 264 (1859). In addition, see *Congressional Globe*, 35th Cong., 2d sess., 970 (1859) (remarks of Rep. Clark); ibid., 31st Cong., 1st sess., app. 288 (1850) (remarks of Sen. Butler).

sovereignty. Under this test, free blacks clearly qualified as citizens—a point that was recognized by some slave-state courts in the early nineteenth century.[79]

Further, even if one could specify a set of rights that was necessarily appurtenant to citizenship, defining citizenship by reference to these rights would not have completely solved the Southern problem. The nature of the rights granted to blacks varied greatly even among the free states. Although the legal regime of states such as Indiana was almost as hostile to free blacks as were the slave states themselves, a number of free states allowed blacks to vote even prior to the Civil War. Massachusetts also allowed them to serve as jurors. Thus, if the status of citizenship were derived from the possession of rights, Southern theorists would have had to concede that at least *some* free blacks could claim the protection of the Comity Clause.

Finally, any state-centered approach to federal citizenship had to contend with troubling structural anomalies. By its nature, the constitutional definition of citizenship had only limited significance under the antebellum regime. It had no impact on purely domestic issues—most notably, the relationship between a state and its own citizens. Thus, no definition of federal citizenship could in any way threaten the core principle of state autonomy. What was at stake instead were some of the specific rights entrusted to the federal government by the Constitution. To have state governments control access to those rights necessarily created some tension with the basic idea that the federal government was supreme within its own sphere of influence.

The argument that federal citizenship might be defined separately from state citizenship faced different problems. The structure of Article IV itself seems inconsistent with the notion that a person who is recognized as a citizen by his home state would not

---

79. *State v. Manuel*, 20 N.C. (4 Dev. and Bat). 144 (1838); *Fisher's Negroes v. Dabbs*, 14 Tenn. (6 Yer.) 119 (1834); Kettner, *Development of American Citizenship*, p. 320. In addition, see 4 *Opinions of the Attorney General* 147 (1843).

be entitled to the privileges and immunities guaranteed by the Comity Clause; the Constitution provides that "[t]he Citizens of *each State* shall be entitled to all Privileges and Immunities of Citizens in the several States." Thus, if State A recognizes a resident as a citizen, the language of the Comity Clause seems to require all other states to recognize that citizenship as well. In short, both positions on the citizenship issue faced conceptual problems, and the issue would not be definitively settled until the decision in *Dred Scott*.

The facts of *Dred Scott* have all the complexity of a well-constructed question on a law-school examination.[80] Dred Scott was a slave purchased in Missouri by one Dr. John Emerson. Emerson received a commission in the United States Army and brought Scott with him first to Illinois—a free state—and then to the Wisconsin Territory, an area in which slavery was forbidden by the Missouri Compromise. While at the latter post, with the consent of his master, Scott married a woman named Harriet. After returning to St. Louis, Emerson also married and, upon his death, willed Scott to his widow.

In 1846, Scott began an action in Missouri state court to obtain his freedom, alleging that Emerson had emancipated him by voluntarily taking him to reside in a free state. Under existing Missouri precedent, Scott seemed to have a strong case.[81] However, after a complex legal struggle, the Missouri Supreme Court ruled against him.[82] Scott was then sold to a New York resident and instituted a suit for freedom in federal court, alleging that the jurisdiction of the federal courts could be founded on diversity of citizenship as the basis for federal jurisdiction. It was this second suit that found its way to the Supreme Court as *Dred Scott v. Sandford*.[83]

---

80. The complicated facts of *Dred Scott* are described in detail in Fehrenbacher, *The Dred Scott Case*, pp. 239–284.

81. *Rachel v. Walker*, 4 Mo. 350 (1836).

82. *Scott v. Emerson*, 15 Mo. 576 (1852).

83. 60 U.S. (19 How.) 393 (1857).

Dred Scott is most famous for Chief Justice Roger Brooke Taney's opinion holding that the Missouri Compromise was unconstitutional and that Congress could not outlaw slavery in the territories. However, the case also presented the question of whether blacks could be considered "citizens of the United States" and thus eligible to bring diversity actions in federal court. Speaking for the majority, Taney began his discussion of the citizenship issue by defining the scope of the inquiry in the most sweeping terms. Declining to consider the possibility that the definition of Article III citizenship might be broader than that of federal citizenship for other purposes under the Constitution, he stated: "The question is... Can a negro, whose ancestors were imported into this country and sold as slaves, become a member of the political community formed and brought into existence by the Constitution of the United States and as such become entitled to all the rights, and privileges, and immunities, guarantied by that instrument to the citizen [including] the privilege of suing in a court of the United States?" Taney then differentiated sharply between state citizenship and federal citizenship, contending that while a state could declare anyone it pleased to be a citizen for its own purposes, the states lacked authority to "introduce a new member into the political community created by the Constitution of the United States." That status, according to Taney, was to be determined by a federal standard and limited to members of two groups: (1) "every person, every class and description of persons, who were at the time of the adoption of the Constitution recognized as citizens in the several States," and (2) those foreigners whom Congress might choose to naturalize under the authority granted to it by the Constitution.[84]

Taney next turned to an extended historical discussion of the status of free blacks in the late eighteenth century, beginning with his oft-quoted (and misquoted) observation that "they had no rights which the white man was bound to respect" and conclud-

84. Ibid., pp. 403, 405–406, 422–423, 419, 406, 419–420.

ing that free blacks were not considered citizens. In reaching this conclusion, Taney relied on a number of different sources. First, he argued that the laws of the various states limiting the rights of blacks during the founding period were inconsistent with the status of citizenship. Second, he claimed that the Fugitive Slave Clause and the clause limiting congressional power over the slave trade "point directly and specifically to the negro race as a separate class of persons... not regarded as a portion of the... citizens of the Government [formed by the Constitution]." Third, he contended that early actions of the federal government seemed to reflect the view that free blacks were not citizens. Finally, he argued that during the founding period, many states would have been unwilling to allow transient black inhabitants from other states the privileges and immunities guaranteed to them by the Comity Clause.[85]

In making this argument, Taney invoked elements of both the antidiscrimination and absolute rights theories of the Comity Clause. Initially, he used antidiscrimination language in describing the effect of the clause, declaring that it "gave to each citizen outside of his state... and placed him in every other State on a perfect equality with its own citizens in rights of person and rights of property."[86] However, a pure antidiscrimination analysis would have provided little support for Taney's argument; under this view, states would be required to grant sojourning free blacks only those rights that they granted to free black domiciliaries, who often enjoyed few rights in slave states.

Accordingly, later in the opinion, Taney's rhetoric changed, reflecting an absolute rights view that was nonetheless modified by antidiscrimination concepts. Thus, he asserted that if states were required to recognize sojourning blacks as citizens,

> it would exempt them from the operation of the special laws [and give them the right]... to go where they

85. Ibid., pp. 419–420, 407, 408–409, 412–417, 411, 419–421, 422–423.
86. Ibid., p. 407.

> pleased at every hour of the day or night without molestation, unless they committed some violation of law for which a white man would be punished and... the full liberty of speech in public and in private upon all subjects upon which [the state's] own citizens might speak.[87]

He also contended that

> if [a person] ranks as a citizen of the State to which he belongs, within the meaning of the Constitution of the United States, then, whenever he goes into another State, the Constitution clothes him, as though the rights of person, with all privileges and immunities which belong to citizens of the State. And if persons of the African race are citizens of a State, and of the United States, they would be entitled to all of these privileges and immunities in every State, and the State could not restrict them; for they would hold these privileges and immunities under the paramount authority of the Federal Government, and its courts would be bound to maintain and enforce them, the Constitution and laws of the State to the contrary notwithstanding.[88]

Despite its lack of rigorous theoretical consistency, the discussion of the Comity Clause played an important role in Taney's opinion. However, the significance of the discussion was not so much legal as rhetorical. By emphasizing the rights that he contended would accrue to free blacks if they were to be considered citizens, Taney implicitly associated Dred Scott's supporters with advocacy of "Negro equality"—a view that was anathema to many white Americans in the overtly racist social and political culture of the antebellum era. While the issue of free-black citizenship was analytically separable from the question of the constitutionality of

87. Ibid., pp. 416–417.
88. Ibid., pp. 422–423.

the Missouri Compromise, Taney no doubt hoped that his analysis of the citizenship issue and his use of the Comity Clause would help build public support for his opinion as a whole.

By contrast, the Comity Clause played no role in the dissenting opinion of Justice John McLean. McLean wasted little time in disposing of the citizenship issue. Like Taney, Justice John McLean argued that for constitutional purposes, federal citizenship was to be determined by federal law. However, he took a radically different view of the substantive content of that standard, arguing that "the most general and appropriate definition of the term citizen is 'a freeman.'"[89] Under this view, Scott's jurisdictional allegations clearly met the requirements of both Article III and the jurisdictional statute.

Characteristically, Justice Benjamin Robbins Curtis steered a middle course on the citizenship question. Curtis first took issue with Taney's reading of history, contending that at least five states had granted citizenship to free blacks at the time the Constitution was drafted. Under the Articles of Confederation, these blacks had been entitled to the privileges and immunities of national citizenship. Thus, for Curtis, the question was whether the Constitution had deprived free blacks of their right to citizenship. After first noting that the Constitution by its terms did not define national citizenship, he expressly considered three other possibilities—that Congress possessed the authority to define citizenship, that all free persons born within the United States were to be considered citizens of the United States, and that each State was to be free to determine "what free persons, born within its limits, shall be citizens of such State, and *thereby* citizens of the United States."[90]

Curtis rejected the first possibility on both practical and doctrinal grounds. He initially observed that if Congress possessed such a power, it could unduly circumscribe the class of persons el-

89. Ibid., p. 531.
90. Ibid., pp. 581, 576, 577.

igible to be president, vice president, or members of Congress simply by defining the term "citizen of the United States" narrowly. In addition, he noted that the Constitution does not specifically grant Congress general authority to define citizenship; the only directly relevant provision states that Congress shall have power "to establish a uniform rule of *naturalization*"—a term that, for Curtis (like Taney), was limited to the removal of the disabilities of alienage arising from foreign birth. Therefore, the doctrine of enumerated powers also militated against the theory that Congress had unfettered authority to grant or withhold national citizenship.[91]

Curtis was thus left with a choice between McLean's position—that all native-born free persons were citizens—and the conclusion that each state had the authority to decide (at least as an initial matter) which of its native-born residents should be considered citizens of the United States. In defending the latter theory, Curtis relied in part on a textual argument. He observed that the Comity Clause provides that "citizens of each *State* shall be entitled to all the privileges and immunities of citizens of the several States"—in effect, choosing state citizenship as the benchmark for the determination that a person was entitled to national protection for the rights appurtenant to that status.[92]

Primarily, however, Curtis grounded his conclusion in fundamental principles of constitutional interpretation. He noted that prior to the adoption of the Constitution, each state possessed the authority to define citizenship as an inherent aspect of its sovereign authority. Further, the states retained all aspects of sovereign authority not granted to the federal government by the Constitution. Since only the power of naturalization was granted to Congress, in Curtis's view, the states retained authority to determine the status of native-born residents.[93]

---

91. Ibid., pp. 577–578, 578 (emphasis added).
92. Ibid., p. 580 (emphasis added).
93. Ibid., pp. 578–580.

While rejecting Taney's extreme proslavery approach, this conclusion fell far short of advanced antislavery positions. First, Curtis observed that under his theory, if an African American were born in a state that did not consider him a citizen, he could *never* achieve that status. Moreover, while states did not possess the power to confer national citizenship on persons born outside their borders, Curtis argued that federal power over naturalization extended only to aliens—those born outside the boundaries of the United States. Thus, while in theory Congress could have granted American citizenship to a native African who emigrated to the United States, it was powerless to take similar action with respect to a person who was born a slave in South Carolina and was later emancipated in Massachusetts.[94]

Moreover, under Curtis's approach, the Constitution would guarantee only limited rights to those free blacks who were in fact citizens of the United States. Clearly, as citizens they would be entitled to invoke the jurisdiction of the federal courts on the ground of diversity of citizenship, and to be candidates for president, vice president, and Congress. The Comity Clause also guaranteed citizens of the United States the right to free ingress to and egress from all states in the Union—a right that was denied by the Negro Seamen's Acts. The question of what other rights free black citizens would enjoy, however, would be in considerable measure a function of state law.

In reaching this conclusion, Curtis relied on the dominant view of the Comity Clause, which both limited the scope of the rights covered by the concept of privileges and immunities and, in many cases, defined the rights of sojourners by reference to those granted by the state to its own citizens. Under this view, if a state imposed some racial restriction on its own black citizens, it could impose a similar restriction on blacks from other states. Thus, Curtis had two responses to the argument that, under his approach, states such as South Carolina would be required to

94. Ibid., p. 586.

allow free blacks from (for example) Massachusetts to vote and hold office. Curtis first contended that these rights were not protected by the Comity Clause. He then continued:

> Privileges and immunities which belong to certain citizens of a State, by reason of the operation of causes other than mere citizenship, are not conferred.... It rests with the States themselves so to frame their Constitutions and laws as not to attach a particular privilege or immunity to mere naked citizenship. If one of the State will not deny to any of its citizens a particular privilege or immunity, if it confer it on all of them by reason of mere naked citizenship, then it may be claimed by every citizen of each State by force of the Constitution.[95]

This analysis clearly indicates that states that granted free blacks citizenship could nonetheless place race-based restrictions on the rights of all blacks—whether domiciliaries or sojourners. Suppose, however, that a state restricted citizenship to white domiciliaries. Could it then deny to black citizens from other states a fundamental right that it granted to all white, native-born citizens—for example, the right to buy real property? Although the language of his opinion suggests that such discrimination would be constitutional under the Comity Clause, Curtis did not give a definitive answer to this question.[96]

In any event, Curtis did not prevail. The majority opinion not only implicitly affirmed the constitutionality of the Negro Seamen's Acts but also gave impetus to the efforts of proslavery theorists to turn the Comity Clause to their own advantage. Most often, proslavery theorists argued that the Comity Clause required at least a limited extension of slavery into the free states.

In the wake of *Dred Scott*, one extreme example of such an argument appeared in the proslavery *Washington Union* on Novem-

---

95. Ibid., pp. 583–584.

96. Don E. Fehrenbacher apparently takes a different view. Fehrenbacher, *The Dred Scott Case*, pp. 407–408.

ber 27, 1857. Citing the Comity Clause, the newspaper noted that every citizen of a state was entitled to the protection of his property when he traveled to another state. Relying on *Dred Scott* for the proposition that the Constitution protects property in slaves, the *Union* argued that the privileges and immunities of citizenship included the right of citizens of slave states to migrate and settle in free states and to have their slave property protected in their new homes. Thus, the editorial concluded that free-state laws that deprived slaveholders from slave states of their slaves were unconstitutional.[97]

Even before *Dred Scott*, Southerners relied on the Comity Clause to support a less extreme but more plausible position. In particular, they contended that the Constitution guaranteed slave-owners the right to pass through free states without being deprived of their property. This argument rested on the absolute rights theory of the Comity Clause; slaveholders were claiming a right not available to the citizens of the relevant states—the right to hold slaves. Notwithstanding this difficulty, in 1843, the Illinois Supreme Court accepted the slaveholders' argument in *Willard v. The People*,[98] and Justice Henry Baldwin had made an analogous argument in *Groves v. Slaughter*.[99] Other Northern state courts took a contrary view;[100] however, *Dred Scott*'s holding on slavery in the territories seemed to support the proslavery position.

Summary

In discussing antebellum constitutional theory, commentators normally focus on the differences between the political/legal the-

---

97. The editorial is reproduced in *Congressional Globe*, 35th Cong., 1st sess., app. 199–200 (1858).

98. 4 Ill. (4 Scam.) 461, 471–472 (1843). The California Supreme Court took the same view in *Ex Parte Archy*, 9 Cal. 147 (1858).

99. 40 U.S. (15 Pet.) 449, 515–517 (1841) (opinion of Baldwin, J.).

100. See, for example, *Lemmon v. The People*, 26 N.Y. 270 (1857); *Anderson v. Poindexter*, 6 Ohio St. 623 (1857).

ories underlying the proslavery and antislavery positions. Clearly such differences were significant: antislavery thought was more egalitarian and dependent on natural law theory, while proslavery thought envisioned a more hierarchical society and (at least at times) rejected the concept of natural law. Nonetheless, with respect to the concepts that were to be embodied in section 1—due process, equal protection, and privileges and immunities—the approaches of the two groups reflected substantial similarities.

First, although widely accepted theories of due process analysis would have provided a grounding for classification-based arguments, both antislavery and proslavery analysis generally rested on a theory of absolute rights belonging to every member of the community—what might be described as a theory of limited absolute equality. The difference between the two groups rested on their respective views of the status of a single, discrete class of individuals—slaves. Antislavery advocates considered members of this class to be persons, and as such entitled to the fundamental rights of persons. Proslavery advocates, by contrast, viewed the slaves primarily as property and thus focused on the rights of owners.

On its face, the proslavery equal protection analysis might be viewed as an exception. Seemingly relying on a classification-based theory, this analysis accused the federal government of discriminating against a discrete class of property—slaves—and its owners. The antislavery response, however, was not that the government had a right to discriminate against a class of property owners; instead, it relied on the proposition that slaves in the territories simply had ceased to be property. Thus, the central question was not the appropriateness of discriminating against a category of property, but whether the putative slaves should be defined as property at all. The Reconstruction amendments would give a definitive answer to this question. At the same time, however, they would set in motion a series of events that would require the Supreme Court to reexamine in detail the concepts of due process, equal protection, and privileges and immunities of citizenship.

Chapter 2

The Drafting of the Fourteenth Amendment

Taken as a whole, the Fourteenth Amendment was clearly a political document, designed to present the Republican party's terms for the readmission of the ex-Confederate states. Moreover, section 1 was obviously an integral part of this proposal, expressing the principle that the Southern states must commit themselves to respect and protect the fundamental rights of American citizens generally. At the same time, however, congressional Republicans were acutely aware that section 1 in particular would have a significant impact on legal doctrine. They took considerable care to produce a provision that they hoped would have as few unintended consequences as possible.[1] The evolution of the Citizenship Clause clearly reflects the thoughtfulness with which the framers chose the language of the amendment.

The attitude of the Republican party toward the question of African American citizenship underwent a profound transformation during the Civil War and the early Reconstruction period. During the antebellum era, party members were deeply divided on the issue. As the Civil War progressed, however, Republicans

1. This view is admittedly controversial. For differing assessments, see, for example, Harold M. Hyman and William M. Wiecek, *Equal Justice Under Law: Constitutional Development, 1835–1875* (New York, 1982), ch. 11; Earl M. Maltz, *Civil Rights, the Constitution, and Congress, 1863–1869* (Lawrence, Kan., 1990); William E. Nelson, *The Fourteenth Amendment: From Political Principle to Judicial Doctrine* (Cambridge, Mass., 1988).

began to coalesce around the position taken by Justice Mclean in *Dred Scott.* By the time that the Fourteenth Amendment was drafted, mainstream Republicans almost unanimously embraced the principle that native-born African Americans should be viewed as citizens of the United States.

For many Republicans, this change in position occurred relatively soon after the war began. The shift was signaled by Attorney General Edward Bates's analysis of the status of free blacks in an opinion issued on November 29, 1862. In considering whether African Americans were citizens within the meaning of a federal statute, Bates declared that national citizenship was solely a matter of federal law and that all citizens of the nation were also citizens of the respective states in which they were domiciled. Further, Bates concluded that all native-born free blacks were citizens of the United States, characterizing the contrary conclusion of the majority in *Dred Scott* as "*dehors the record* [i.e., dictum] and of no authority as a judicial decision."[2]

Taken alone, these conclusions might have formed the basis for a claim that states were under an obligation to grant free blacks a variety of basic rights. However, another prominent feature of the opinion was its rejection of the tangible rights theory of citizenship. Bates noted that infants and females were considered citizens despite the fact that they possessed few if any of the rights normally associated with that status; he further observed that even those who were sold into involuntary servitude as a punishment for crime retained their citizenship. Thus he declared, "I can hardly comprehend the thought of the absolute incompatibility of degradation and citizenship." Drawing on authorities such as Kent and Blackstone, Bates espoused a quite different definition of citizenship:

> In my opinion, the Constitution uses the word citizen only to express the political quality of the individual

2. 10 *Opinions of the Attorney General* 382, 388, 412 (1862) (emphasis in original).

> in his relations to the nation; to declare that he is a member of the body politic, and bound to it by the reciprocal obligation of allegiance on the one side and protection on the other.

Bates explicitly concluded that this right to "protection" was not inconsistent with the denial of important rights.[3] Thus, in isolation at least, the practical significance of the Bates opinion was quite limited.

In other respects, however, the opinion was profoundly significant. Although Bates's conclusions were not immediately accepted by all Republicans—as late as 1864, its premises were questioned by Republican senators such as John Henderson of Missouri and Peter Van Winkle of West Virginia[4]—the attorney general spoke as the official voice of the Lincoln administration, and thus for the national Republican party itself. Moreover, despite the narrowness of the opinion, in symbolic terms it recognized free blacks as equal members of American society. Thus, in a limited sense at least, the opinion clearly committed the Republican party to the principle of racial equality.

Given racial attitudes in 1862, such a commitment carried substantial political risks. Republicans were well aware of these risks;[5] indeed, the issuance of the opinion (three weeks *after* the elections of 1862) was no doubt timed to minimize damage to Republican candidates. However, the Lincoln administration was willing to take these risks as part of the ongoing effort to discredit *Dred Scott*. This effort was critical to the theoretical justification for Lincoln's military response to secession. If the majority opinion on the issue of slavery in the territories had in fact been an authoritative, binding interpretation of the Constitution, then secession was a response to the refusal by the federal government to

---

3. Ibid., pp. 408, 398, 388, 398–399, 407–408.
4. *Congressional Globe*, 38th Cong., 1st sess., 1459–1465 (1864) (Henderson); ibid., pp. 1780–1781 (Van Winkle).
5. See, for example, *The New York Times*, Dec. 17, 1862, p. 4, col. 4.

recognize the legitimate interests of the slave states—at worst, a rebellion against unjust governmental action. This was hardly the background against which Republicans sought to prosecute the war effort.

Of course, in theory Republicans might have focused their attacks entirely on the territorial question, simply ignoring Taney's treatment of the citizenship issue; indeed, this was the approach taken by many antislavery commentators immediately after *Dred Scott* was decided. In the public mind, however, the two aspects of the decisions were linked. Thus, in the words of *The New York Times*, "[I]t was incumbent upon the [Lincoln] Administration to purge the Government of all recognition of [the doctrines of *Dred Scott*] on the first fair opportunity."[6]

Lincoln's prewar response to the citizenship problem rested on the view that national citizenship was derived from state citizenship. Prior to the outbreak of the Civil War, this view was shared by many in the antislavery movement. However, after secession, the state-centered view created conceptual difficulties for Union theorists. This view of citizenship was not entirely compatible with the position that states had no right to leave the Union and that support for the Confederate cause was treason. Against this background, the most plausible response to Taney's opinion was to adopt Justice McLean's position in *Dred Scott* and argue that all native-born free blacks were citizens of the Union. In any event, the Bates opinion marked an important stage in the evolution of the Republican attitude toward citizenship. The next major turning point came in the drafting of the Civil Rights Act of 1866.

As initially proposed by Senator Lyman Trumbull of Illinois on January 5, 1866, section 1 of the Civil Rights Act of 1866 did not deal with citizenship at all. Instead, the Bill stated:

> There shall be no discrimination in civil rights or im-

---

6. Fehrenbacher, *The Dred Scott Case*, ch. 18; *The New York Times*, Dec. 17, 1862, p. 4, col. 4.

> munities among the *inhabitants* of any state or Territory of the United States on account of race, color, or previous condition of slavery; but the inhabitants of every race and color, without regard to any previous condition of slavery or involuntary servitude... shall have the same right to make and enforce contracts, to sue, to be parties and to give evidence, to inherit, purchase, lease, sell, hold, and convey real and personal property, and to full and equal benefits of all laws and proceedings for the security of persons and property and shall be subject to like punishment, pains and penalties, and to none other.

Congressional power to pass the proposal in this form could only be found in the enforcement clause of the Thirteenth Amendment. Reliance on this constitutional provision posed substantial problems. First, one had to conclude that the Thirteenth Amendment went beyond mere dissolution of the master/slave relationship and granted Congress the authority to protect a certain class of rights that was essential to the status of freedman. Substantial evidence supports the conclusion that this position was consistent with the understanding of the drafters of the Thirteenth Amendment;[7] nonetheless, from the language of the amendment, the grant of such power is far from clear.

Moreover, even if one conceded that the Thirteenth Amendment vested power in Congress to protect certain rights, some of the prohibitions in the Civil Rights Bill might have been considered to be beyond that power. Some Republicans believed that the section 2 authority extended only to those rights which were essential to the status of a freedman. Put another way, if one could be a freedman without a particular right, then Congress could not rely on Thirteenth Amendment authority to protect that right. Although aliens, for example, were clearly not slaves,

---

7. Earl M. Maltz, *Civil Rights, the Constitution and Congress, 1863–1869* (Lawrence, Kan., 1990), ch. 2.

they had historically been limited in their right to own real property and to inherit intestate. Thus, one could be deprived of those rights and yet not have the status of a slave.[8] Nonetheless, both rights were protected by Trumbull's proposal.

To address this problem, even before the bill was debated in the full Senate, Trumbull moved an amendment to provide that "all persons of African descent born in the United States are hereby declared to be citizens of the United States." Soon thereafter, the language was altered to provide that "all persons born in the United States and not subject to any foreign power" were to be deemed citizens. Trumbull argued that the Naturalization Clause as well as the Thirteenth Amendment gave Congress authority to adopt this provision. He further contended that the power to create citizens necessarily implied a power to guarantee that the states would ensure the rights of citizens to the naturalized persons or groups. These rights he defined by reference to judicial decisions interpreting the Comity Clause. Other prominent Republicans argued that the Comity Clause itself conferred authority on Congress to protect the "privileges and immunities" of all citizens.[9] Both of these assertions were controversial; nonetheless, the relationship between the citizens of the United States and the federal government became the anchor to which the Civil Rights Bill was attached.

Democrats attacked the citizenship provision, contending that blacks should not be made citizens and that, in any event, *Dred Scott* could only be overruled by a constitutional amendment. Republicans generally rejected these arguments. At the same time, however, they showed considerable concern about the proper limitations on "the inestimable privilege" of American citizenship and the rights appurtenant to that status.[10] Republicans were par-

---

8. See, for example, *Congressional Globe*, 39th Cong., 1st sess., app. 158 (1866).

9. Ibid., pp. 475, 499–500, 600.

10. Ibid., p. 527 (remarks of Sen. Ramsey).

ticularly concerned with the impact of the proposed language on the position of Native Americans.

The parameters of the status of Native Americans were clearly established in the antebellum era. Native Americans were viewed as owing allegiance to their tribal governments rather than to the government of the United States. Thus, they typically did not acquire American citizenship simply by virtue of being born within the territorial limits of the United States. Moreover, under the terms of the naturalization statutes, Native Americans were generally ineligible for naturalization. Nonetheless, some groups of Native Americans and their descendants acquired citizenship by virtue of treaties and specific statutory authorization.[11] Neither party wished to change these established principles.

Against this background, Trumbull's formulation generated consternation that cut across party lines. Both Democratic Senator James Guthrie of Kentucky and radical Republican Senator Jacob Howard of Michigan expressed the fear that Trumbull's proposal would naturalize all Native Americans. Trumbull responded that this was not his intention. Noting that the Indian tribes were viewed as separate nations, Trumbull argued that his proposal would only grant citizenship to those Indians "who are domesticated and pay taxes and live in civilized society" and thus had become "incorporated into the United States." Nonetheless, he indicated a willingness to include a provision dealing specifically with Native American citizenship.[12]

At this point, Republican Senator Henry Lane of Kansas raised the issue of the status of Native Americans who had taken individual allotments of land as provided by treaty. While Trumbull insisted that these Native Americans were already citizens, Lane disagreed. To resolve any ambiguities, Lane proposed an amendment that would specifically confer citizenship on "Indians holding lands in severalty by allotment." Trumbull objected

---

11. The status of Native Americans in the antebellum United States is discussed in detail in Kettner, *Development of American Citizenship*.

12. *Congressional Globe*, 39th Cong., 1st sess., 527 (1866).

to this proposal on the ground that some of these allotments remained wholly within the jurisdiction of the tribal government. Thus, the amendment was rejected.[13]

Seeking to deal with the same problem that troubled Lane, Republican Senator Samuel C. Pomeroy of Kansas then proposed to amend the bill to exclude "persons . . . subject to . . . tribal authority" from its declaration of citizenship. This language was ambiguous; it was unclear whether a person who was born subject to tribal authority and later left his tribe to assimilate into white society would become a citizen. Taking the view that such a person would not become a citizen because he was born subject to tribal authority, Democratic Senator Reverdy Johnson of Maryland argued that the Pomeroy language would not solve the problem of Native Americans who took allotments. Disagreeing with Johnson on the import of the language, Guthrie raised a different objection. Focusing on the potential burdens associated with citizenship, he observed that, while immigrants seeking naturalization were required to affirmatively evince a desire to become American citizens, as written, the Civil Rights Bill conferred citizenship *by operation of law* on some classes of Native Americans who had not been born citizens. Guthrie declared, "I cannot consent to impose citizenship and its liabilities upon a people without their assent [or the assent of their government]."[14]

Republican Senators John Conness of California and Alexander Ramsey of Minnesota then raised still another objection to Pomeroy's formulation. They noted that not all Native Americans were associated with a recognizable tribe. Some lived on so-called public reservations, while others traveled in small nomadic groups. Conness and Ramsey pointed out that these nonaligned Native Americans owed no allegiance to any other government. Thus, in their view, by its terms the Pomeroy language would make these Native Americans citizens.[15]

13. Ibid., pp. 498–499, 522, 525, 526.
14. Ibid., pp. 525–526.
15. Ibid., pp. 526–527.

The existence of this class of Native Americans presented Republicans with a conceptual dilemma. As persons who were born within the territorial limits of the United States owing no allegiance to any other government, they were theoretically entitled to citizenship under the dominant Republican ideology of the early Reconstruction era. As Republican Senator John B. Henderson observed, to decide otherwise would be to conclude that "[the government] is made for the white man and the black man, but not the red man." Nonetheless, most Republicans balked at conferring citizenship on a group that they viewed as "perhaps the lowest class known as Indians." Republican Senator George H. Williams of Oregon expressed concern over the extent of the rights that might be granted to these Native Americans if they were made citizens by the proposed Act. He noted that states typically banned sales of firearms and alcoholic beverages to Indians and observed that, under the terms of the bill, states would apparently be powerless to enforce such bans against Indians who were granted citizenship.[16]

This argument bears an almost eerie similarity to Taney's warnings against the dangers of black citizenship in *Dred Scott.* Williams's emphasis on the sale of firearms is particularly striking. One of the common Republican complaints about the Black Codes, whose passage had precipitated the Civil Rights Bill, was that they often prevented free blacks from obtaining firearms.[17] Nonetheless, Williams was apparently in favor of denying to Native Americans what was then viewed as an essential tool of self-protection.

In the face of the Republican objections to the Pomeroy language, Trumbull finally retreated to the phraseology used in the original Constitution, excluding "Indians not taxed" from the de-

---

16. Ibid., pp. 574, 527, 574, 573.

17. *Dred Scott,* 60 U.S. at 416–417; *Congressional Globe,* 39th Cong., 1st sess., 651 (1866) (remarks of Rep. Grinnell); ibid., p. 474 (remarks of Sen. Trumbull).

finition of citizenship in the Civil Rights Bill.[18] Democratic Senator Thomas A. Hendricks of Indiana complained that the right to citizenship should not depend on whether a person pays taxes;[19] Trumbull responded that he was in essence using the phrase as a term of art, connoting "a class of persons who . . . are not regarded as part of our people."[20] Whatever their private reservations, mainstream Republicans proved willing to acquiesce in this formulation, and it became law when the Civil Rights Act as a whole eventually was passed over the veto of President Andrew Johnson.

The passage of the Civil Rights Act did not, however, end the controversy over Indian citizenship. Seeking to definitively overrule *Dred Scott*, Republicans proposed to include language in the Fourteenth Amendment that declared, "All persons born or naturalized in the United States, and subject to the jurisdiction thereof, are citizens of the United States and the State wherein they reside." Senator James R. Doolittle of Wisconsin—a nominal Republican who was by this point firmly allied with the Democrats—proposed to add language that, like the Civil Rights Act, excluded "Indians not taxed" from the definition of citizenship.[21] This language had been adopted by Republicans in section 2 of the proposed amendment, which redefined the basis of representation in the House of Representatives. Nonetheless, clearly having rethought the issue carefully, mainstream Republicans unanimously rejected the idea of incorporating a specific exclusion for Native Americans in the section 1 definition of citizenship.

Both Lyman Trumbull and Jacob Howard, the floor manager of the Fourteenth Amendment in the Senate, argued that the clause as written required Indians to be subject to the "complete" jurisdiction of the United States in order to claim citizenship and thus excluded Indians who retained allegiance to their tribal gov-

---

18. Ibid., p. 527.
19. Ibid.
20. Ibid., pp. 527, 572.
21. Ibid., p. 2892.

ernments. In addition, Trumbull noted that Hendricks's argument against the language of the Civil Rights Act had persuaded him that judges might interpret the phrase "Indians not taxed" literally, thus discriminating between poor Indians and rich Indians in determining citizenship status. Finally, both Howard and Republican Senator Daniel Clark noted that the "Indians not taxed" language in essence gave states the authority to decide whether to naturalize or not naturalize Indians through their taxing policy—an idea that was fundamentally inconsistent with the Republican view that national citizenship should be paramount. Thus, the Doolittle amendment was rejected on a party-line vote,[22] and the definition of citizenship was ultimately adopted without change.

The debate over the proper form of the Citizenship Clause clearly demonstrates that Republicans understood that the specific language chosen for the Fourteenth Amendment would have important legal consequences. The discussions of the remainder of section 1 reflect a similar understanding. Section 1 had its genesis in an effort by John Bingham to remedy what he saw as a specific problem with existing legal doctrine. He first adverted to the need for a constitutional amendment on January 9, 1866. Reiterating his idiosyncratic view of the Comity Clause and referring specifically to the Samuel Hoar affair, Bingham called for an amendment "giving to Congress the power to pass all laws necessary to secure to all persons... their equal personal rights."[23]

Few if any Republicans completely shared Bingham's view of the Constitution. Nonetheless, they faced a related problem of legal uncertainty. By early 1866, all mainstream Republicans were committed to the view that federal action was needed to protect the newly freed slaves from the predations of the Black Codes that had been adopted in many Southern states. They united around the Civil Rights Act of 1866, which prohibited the states from

22. Ibid., pp. 2892, 2893, 2895, 2894, 2895, 2897.
23. Ibid., p. 158.

denying fundamental rights to African Americans. However, as we have already seen, the source of constitutional authority for this statute was uncertain; though some relied on the enforcement clause of the Thirteenth Amendment, and others cited the Comity Clause, neither provision unambiguously provided Congress with authority to pass the necessary legislation. By contrast, a constitutional amendment along the lines of that originally suggested by Bingham would remove all doubt on this issue.

Against this background, at Bingham's urging, the Joint Committee on Reconstruction proposed the following constitutional amendment:

> The Congress shall have power to make all laws which shall be necessary and proper to secure to the citizens of each State all privileges and immunities of citizens of the several states and to all persons in the several States equal protection in the rights of life, liberty and property.

This proposal engendered a lively debate on the floor of the House of Representatives. Democrats unanimously rejected the view that the Constitution should be changed. Republicans, by contrast, were split. While some supported the Bingham amendment, others believed that its equal protection component was both unnecessary and dangerous.

Throughout the debate, both sides emphasized the legal import of the Bingham language. For example, in his capacity as floor manager of the proposal, Bingham explained that its language was drawn from the Comity Clause and the Due Process Clause of the Fifth Amendment. When Democratic Representative Andrew Rogers of New Jersey challenged Bingham to explain the legal import of the Due Process Clause, Bingham replied dismissively that "the courts have settled that long ago, and the gentleman can go and read their decisions."[24] Thus he implicitly but

24. Ibid., p. 1089.

clearly recognized the distinctively legal import of the proposal as well as the belief that interpretation would be based upon the principles of ordinary legal analysis.

Against this background, those who attacked the Bingham proposal made a number of different arguments. Republican Representative Giles W. Hotchkiss of New York argued that, rather than relying only on congressional action, the amendment should also directly prohibit the states from infringing on fundamental rights. More often, however, the critics of the proposed amendment criticized its breadth. Some questioned the necessity of providing any additional constitutional protection for fundamental rights. Others contended that the proposal would unduly expand the powers of the federal government. Bingham found it relatively easy to respond to the first objection (at least to the satisfaction of his Republican colleagues); challenged to cite a case in which the Constitution had been pronounced to be "insufficient," he seized upon the Supreme Court's decisions in *Barron v. City of Baltimore* and *Livingston's Lessee v. Moore*, both of which concluded that the Bill of Rights did not limit actions taken by state governments. He bolstered his argument by citing a variety of other mainstream legal sources, including *McCulloch v. Maryland*, *Gibbons v. Ogden*, Joseph Story's *Commentaries on the Constitution*, and James Kent's *Commentaries on American Law*, in order to emphasize the basic point that the federal government was one of enumerated powers that, absent an explicit grant of authority, could not intervene to protect the fundamental rights of citizens.[25]

The debate over the second objection was far more complex. Republicans who opposed Bingham on this ground based their objection on a close reading of the equal protection language in the committee proposal. Thus, for example, Republican Representative Thomas T. Davis of New York contended,

> An amendment which gives in terms to Congress the

25. Ibid., pp. 1089, app. 133, 1089–1090, 1094.

> power to make all laws necessary and proper to secure to every citizen in the several states equal protection in life, liberty and property, is a grant of original jurisdiction to Congress. If Congress may give equal protection to all as to property, it is itself the judge of that protection. Its legislation may be universal. It may enlarge protection, it may circumscribe it and limit it, if only it make it equal.[26]

Similarly, Republican Representative Robert S. Hale of New York stated that "in its grammatical and legal construction" the proposal

> is a grant of the fullest and most ample power to Congress to make all laws "necessary and proper to secure to all persons in the several States protection in the rights of life, liberty and property," with the simple proviso that such protection shall be equal. It is not a mere provision that when the States undertake to give protection which is unequal Congress may equalize it; it is a grant of power in general terms—a grant of the right to legislate for the protection of life, liberty and property, simply qualified by the condition that it shall be equal legislation.[27]

Hale bolstered this argument with a reference to the legal standard established in *McCulloch v. Maryland*:

> It has been settled judicially, as well as legislatively, that the words "necessary and proper," which are found in this amendment, as well as in the original Constitution, by no means imply indispensable necessity; that the legislation "necessary" for carrying into execution powers is not the legislation without

---

26. Ibid., p. 1087.
27. Ibid., p. 1063. To the same effect, see the remarks of Republican Senator William M. Stewart of Nevada, ibid., p. 1082.

> which the thing cannot be done. But it has been expressly settled that it means simply "needful," "requisite," "conducive to."[28]

Hale also used the example of married women's property rights as a specific illustration of his point:

> Take the case of married women; did any one ever assume that Congress was to be invested with the power to legislate on that subject, and to say that married women, in regard to their rights of property, should stand on the same footing with men and unmarried women? There is not a State in the Union where disability of married women in relation to the rights of property does not exist to a greater or lesser extent.[29]

As has often been noted, Thaddeus Stevens of Pennsylvania responded, "When a distinction is made between two married people or two *femmes soles*, that is unequal legislation; but where all of the same class are dealt with in the same way there is no pretense of inequality." Hale, however, refused to accept this explanation:

> [I]f [the language of the proposal] means you shall extend to one married woman the same protection you extend to another, and not the same you extend to unmarried women and men, then by parity of reasoning it will be sufficient if you extend to one negro the same rights you do to another, but not those you extend to a white man.[30]

Bingham's response to Hale on this issue—delivered the next day—is less often considered:

28. Ibid., p. 1065.
29. Ibid., p. 1064.
30. Ibid.

> [Representative Hale says] if you adopt this amendment you give to Congress the power to enforce all the rights of married women in the several States.... He need not be alarmed at the condition of married women. Those rights which are universal and independent of all local State legislation belong, by the gift of God, to every woman, whether married or single. The rights of life and liberty are theirs whatever States may enact. But the gentleman's concern is as to the right of property in married women.
>
> Although this word property has been in your Bill of Rights from the year 1789 until this hour, who ever heard it intimated that anybody could have property protected in any state until he owned or acquired property there according to its local law or according to the law of some other State which he may have carried thither? I undertake to say no one.
>
> As to real estate, everyone knows that its acquisition and transmission under every interpretation ever given to the word property as used in the Constitution of the country are dependent exclusively upon the local law of the State, save under a direct grant of the United States. But suppose any person has acquired property not contrary to the laws of the State but in accordance with its law, are they not to be equally protected in the enjoyment of it, or are they to be denied all protection? That is the question, and the whole question, so far as that part of the case is concerned.

Pressed further by Hale on this point, Bingham then cited the Supreme Court's decision in *Groves v. Slaughter* to illustrate the point that the right to hold personal as well as real property was solely a function of state law.[31]

---

31. Ibid., pp. 1089, 1094. Other discussions of the exchange between Hale, Stevens, and Bingham include Baer, *Equality under the Constitution*, p. 90;

Obviously, Hale and Bingham differed radically on their understanding of the scope of the proposed constitutional amendment. However, both men clearly understood that, if adopted, the proposal would have a significant impact on legal doctrine. They also implicitly acknowledged that the import of that change would be determined by the distinctive principles of legal analysis, including reference to established mainstream legal authorities. The only difference between them was in their interpretation of the relevant authorities.

In any event, arguments such as Hale's obviously had a significant effect on the evolution of the Fourteenth Amendment. Faced with the opposition of men such as Davis and Hale, Bingham and his supporters realized that they could not possibly muster the two-thirds majority necessary to have the amendment adopted. Thus, all mainstream Republicans acquiesced in a motion to have Bingham's proposal referred back to the Joint Committee on Reconstruction. When the proposal reemerged as part of the omnibus Fourteenth Amendment, two important changes in language had been made. First, as Hotchkiss had suggested, a direct prohibition on state action had been added to the grant of congressional power. Second, the grant of power to guarantee "equal protection in the rights of life, liberty and property," to which Hale, Davis, and others had objected, was replaced by a guarantee that these rights would not be abridged without "due process of law" and that the states would grant to all persons "equal protection of the laws." As we have seen, unlike the open-ended language of the proposal that had originally come to the floor, antebellum legal authorities had clearly established relatively narrow meanings for both of the new clauses. The change in phraseology apparently mollified conservative mainstream Republicans such as Hale and Davis, who made no objection to the modified language.

Alexander M. Bickel, "The Original Understanding and the Segregation Decisions," *Harvard Law Review* 69 (1955): 1–65, p. 30.

Indeed, most of the congressional debate over the proposed Fourteenth Amendment did not focus on section 1 at all, but rather on sections 2 and 3, which did not directly purport to protect individual rights at all. Focusing primarily on the Privileges and Immunities Clause, Democrats did argue that the proposal swept too broadly, with some contending in particular that section 1 would require states to enfranchise African Americans.[32] Republicans—some with regret—uniformly denied this assertion.

The most extensive analysis of section 1 came from Republican Senator Jacob M. Howard, a well-respected constitutional authority. Because of the illness of Republican Senator William Pitt Fessenden, the chairman of the Joint Committee on Reconstruction, Howard became the floor manager of the Fourteenth Amendment in the Senate. The bulk of his presentation was devoted to an analysis of the Citizenship Clause and the Privileges and Immunities Clause, which were generally regarded as the linchpins of section 1. Though he conceded that the precise scope of the Privileges and Immunities Clause was unclear at the margins, he also insisted that the scope of the Clause could be divined from existing legal sources such as the Bill of Rights and the Comity Clause. In particular, he cited Bushrod Washington's opinion in *Corfield v. Coryell* as the canonical source for the interpretation of section 1.[33]

However, notwithstanding the fact that Washington had idiosyncratically contended that the right to vote was subsumed in the Comity Clause, Howard joined his Republican colleagues in firmly rejecting the suggestion that section 1 would enfranchise African Americans. In defending this conclusion, Howard, like other Republicans, relied on the distinction between fundamental rights and conventional rights that was a hallmark of antebellum jurisprudence.

---

32. See, for example, the remarks of Democratic Representative Andrew J. Rogers of New Jersey, in *Congressional Globe*, 39th Cong., 1st sess., 2538 (1866).

33. Ibid., p. 2765–2767.

> The first section of the proposed amendment does not give [anyone] the right of voting. The right of suffrage is not, in law, one of the privileges and immunities... secured by the Constitution. It is merely the creature of law. It has always been regarded in this country as the result of positive local law, not regarded as one of those fundamental rights lying at the basis of all society.[34]

Taking the same view of the relationship between section 1 and voting rights, Bingham appealed to the legal principle that the language of a document must be read in the context of the whole document, observing that section 2 of the amendment, which readjusted the basis of state representation in the House of Representatives, "excludes the possibility that by the first section suffrage is subjected to congressional law."[35]

Howard and Bingham's treatment of the suffrage issue fits comfortably into the overall pattern of the debate over section 1 of the Fourteenth Amendment. While the political goals of the amendment were those of the antislavery movement, congressional Republicans consistently took the view that the language of section 1 should be interpreted by reference to the principles of ordinary legal analysis. In this context, they viewed the theory of limited absolute equality as the centerpiece of that analysis. Thus, the original focus of the amendment was not the abolition of racial discrimination per se, but rather the protection of fundamental rights generally. However, ultimately the judicial interpretation of the Fourteenth Amendment in the late nineteenth century would turn the amendment in a quite different direction.

---

34. Ibid, p. 2766.
35. Ibid., p. 2542.

Chapter 3

Refining the Definition of Citizenship

As the previous chapter demonstrated, one of the goals of the drafters of section 1 of the Fourteenth Amendment was to overrule *Dred Scott* and firmly establish the principle of birthright citizenship. The language chosen quite clearly accomplished that objective in general terms. However, at the margins at least, some doubts about the scope of the definition of citizenship remained. It was left to the Supreme Court to resolve those doubts.

The first citizenship-related issue that came to the Court after the ratification of the amendment involved the status of Native Americans. Despite the careful drafting effort of Trumbull and his colleagues, the Citizenship Clause did not resolve all ambiguities on this issue. One such ambiguity involved the status of Native Americans who chose not to live on reservations. Plainly, a Native American who was born on a reservation and remained there was not made a citizen of the United States by the Fourteenth Amendment. However, the language did not clearly establish the status of a Native American who was born on a reservation, and then voluntarily severed his ties with his tribe and sought to live in white society.

Elk v. Wilkins provided a definitive resolution of this issue. *Elk* arose from the situation of a Native American who had voluntarily separated himself from his tribe and then attempted to vote in the state of Nebraska. If Elk had become a citizen of the United States, the Fifteenth Amendment would prohibit the state from denying him the right to vote because of his race; by contrast, if he was not a citizen, the Fifteenth Amendment gave him no protection. Thus, the key question in the case was whether section 1 of the Fourteenth Amendment automatically made Elk a citizen when he moved off the reservation and severed his tribal connection.[1]

Speaking for the majority, Justice Horace Gray concluded that *Elk* was not a citizen and could therefore constitutionally be denied the right to vote in state elections. Gray began with the premise that one could only become a citizen by virtue of either birth or naturalization. Mirroring Trumbull's analysis, Gray noted that, at the time of his birth, Elk was subject to the jurisdiction of an Indian tribe, which Gray described as "an alien, though dependent, power," and could therefore not claim birthright citizenship in the United States. Since Elk had never been naturalized, in Gray's view he failed both tests for citizenship—a conclusion Gray supported by reference to a variety of historical evidence that suggested that Indians born subject to tribal jurisdiction could only obtain citizenship through naturalization.[2]

In his dissent, Justice John Marshall Harlan argued that the legislative history of both the Civil Rights Act of 1866 and the Fourteenth Amendment itself suggested that Elk should be considered a citizen of the United States. He also made a textual argument, noting that section 1 by its terms did not require that persons be "born subject" to the jurisdiction of the United States and that, by leaving his tribe, Elk had become subject to the "complete jurisdiction" of the United States. Moreover, Harlan asserted that, because Indian land should be deemed part of the United States, Elk had been born within the country. These two factors led Harlan to the conclusion that Elk had satisfied the requirements of the Fourteenth Amendment and should therefore be considered an American citizen.[3]

---

1. 112 U.S. 94 (1884).
2. Ibid., pp. 101, 102, 103–109.
3. Ibid., pp. 112–119, 121–122 (Harlan, J., dissenting).

Because it dealt with only a small class of Native Americans, the *Elk* decision was of little political moment. However, *Wong Kim Ark v. United States* was decided in a quite different atmosphere. In *Wong Kim Ark*, the Court was called upon to adjudicate the status of a child of Chinese ancestry who was born in the United States. By its nature, the decision implicated one of the most politically volatile issues of the late nineteenth century.[4]

The situation of the Chinese in America during the late nineteenth century bears some fairly obvious similarities to that of free blacks in the antebellum and early Reconstruction periods. First, both groups were racial minorities, considered inferior by whites, and subjected to discriminatory treatment. For example, the Oregon Constitution of 1857 barred any "Chinaman" who might later arrive in the state from holding real estate and working mining claims, while California both barred the Chinese from testifying in court and imposed discriminatory taxes upon them. Even prior to the adoption of the Fourteenth Amendment, laws that directly interfered with the immigration of Chinese people were routinely held unconstitutional as inconsistent with federal power to regulate foreign commerce; however, the antebellum Constitution posed no bar to measures that sharply curtailed the rights of native Chinese who were already resident in the United States.[5]

Like the defense of black rights, opposition to anti-Chinese measures carried a substantial risk of alienating important groups of white voters. Not surprisingly, the risks were greatest on the Pacific Coast, where the vast majority of Chinese were located

---

4. The discussion that follows is taken from Earl M. Maltz, "The Federal Government and the Problem of Chinese Rights in the Era of the Fourteenth Amendment," *Harvard Journal of Law and Public Policy* 17 (1994): 223–249.

5. Oregon Constitution of 1857, art. 15, sec. 8, reprinted in Benjamin Poore, comp., *The Federal and State Constitutions, Colonial Charters, and Other Organic Laws of the United States*, 2 vols. (Washington, D.C., 1877), 2:1505; *Lin Wang v. Washburn*, 20 Cal. 534 (1862); *People v. Downer*, 7 Cal. 169 (1857); *People v. Hall*, 4 Cal. 399 (1854).

during the Reconstruction era. The California elections of 1867 provided a spectacular example of the importance of the Chinese issue in the far west. Prior to 1867, Republicans were firmly in control of the California state government. However, in that year, an aggressive anti-Chinese posture was the keystone of a Democratic campaign that swept the Republicans from office.[6]

Though the Far West was the epicenter of anti-Chinese sentiment, Stuart C. Miller has demonstrated that the awareness of and distaste for Chinese immigrants was in fact a nationwide phenomenon reflected in the eastern as well as the western press even prior to the Reconstruction era. Eastern reaction to Chinese immigration intensified in the late 1860s and early 1870s, with attempts to establish small groups of Chinese in areas east of the Rocky Mountains and the extensive circulation of a published letter by Henry George warning that the influx of Chinese posed a danger to American society generally.[7] Thus, just as the debate over the proper treatment of African Americans spilled over into other contexts, the political implications of the Chinese question reached well beyond the borders of California, Oregon, and Nevada.

At the same time, a number of important factors also differentiated the situation of the Chinese from that of free blacks. First, the political context of the debate over Chinese rights differed fundamentally from that dealing with the condition of African Americans. Republican advocacy of black rights was not based simply on moral condemnation of racial discrimination; it was

---

6. Elmer Sandmeyer, *The Anti-Chinese Movement in California* (Urbana, Ill., 1939); Alexander P. Saxton, *The Indispensable Enemy: Labor and the Anti-Chinese Movement in California* (Berkeley, 1972), pp. 80–91.

7. Stuart C. Miller, *The Unwelcome Immigrant: The American Image of the Chinese, 1785–1882* (Berkeley, 1969); Gunther Barth, *Bitter Strength: A History of the Chinese in the United States, 1850–1870* (Cambridge, Mass., 1964), pp. 183–213; Frederick Rudolph, "Chinamen in Yankeedom: Anti-Unionism in Massachusetts in 1870," *American Historical Review* 53 (1947): 1–23; Henry George, "The Chinese on the Pacific Coast," *New York Tribune*, May 1, 1869.

also closely intertwined with the struggle with Southern whites for political supremacy. In the antebellum era, Republicans saw the institution of slavery as the cornerstone of the "slave power"—a group of slaveholding whites who sought to control the national government, and to use that government to advance values antithetical to Republican philosophy. After the Civil War, Republicans viewed the empowerment of the free African Americans of the South as a necessary counterweight to the threat of what they saw as a still-unrepentant white populace. By contrast, while advocacy of Chinese rights was viewed by some as generally consistent with basic Republican political and economic philosophy, it did not directly implicate such overarching issues of national power.[8]

The situation of the Chinese was also complicated by factors not presented by that of free African Americans. First, unlike African Americans, whom many whites viewed as having been at least partially Americanized by their lifelong presence in the United States, the Chinese were viewed as having a culture that was fundamentally different from that of American society. Occasionally, influential Republicans described Chinese culture in flattering terms. For example, comparing them favorably with natives of Africa, Republican Senator Lyman Trumbull of Illinois described the Chinese as "citizens from that country which in many respects excels any other country on the face of the globe in the arts and sciences, among whose population are to be found the most learned and eminent scholars in the world."[9] More often, however, the Chinese worldview was portrayed as antithetical to American values.

One of the most potent, recurrent attacks on the Chinese was based on American perceptions of their religion. For example, Republican Senator Henry W. Corbett of Oregon described the

---

8. *The New York Times*, June 26, 1869, p. 4, col. 4; William M. Armstrong, "Godkin and Chinese Labor: A Paradox in Nineteenth Century Liberalism," *American Journal of Economics and Sociology* 21 (1962): 91–108.

9. *Congressional Globe*, 40th Cong., 3d sess., 1036 (1869).

Chinese as "a pagan nation [who] worships their god 'Josh' [*sic*], a god made of wood," and argued that if Chinese were granted full participation in American society, "you may soon find established pagan institutions in our midst which may eventually supersede those Christian influences which so long have been the pride of our country." During the debate over the original formulation of the Fourteenth Amendment, Republican Representative William Higby of California was even more expansive in his condemnation:

> The Chinese are nothing but a pagan race.... You cannot make good citizens of them; they do not learn the language of the country; and you can communicate with them only with the greatest difficulty, as their language is the most difficult of all those spoken; they even dig up their dead while decaying in their graves, strip the putrid flesh from the bones, and transport the bones back to China. They even bring their clay and wooden gods with them.... Judging from the daily exhibition in our streets, and the well-established repute among their females, virtue is an exception to the general rule. They trade their women like cattle, and the trade is mostly for the purpose of prostitution. That is their character.[10]

Higby's tirade also emphasized another important difference between the Chinese and free African Americans—the perception that the Chinese lacked any permanent connection with the United States. By 1866, virtually every black person in the nation was not only a permanent resident but also a native of this country. By contrast, almost all of the Chinese in America had been born in China; they were generally viewed as transients whose loyalties remained with China and who intended to return there.

This difference in country of origin also had an important impact on the legal status of the Chinese in America. Since almost

---

10. Ibid., p. 929; *Congressional Globe*, 39th Cong., 1st sess., 1056 (1866).

all persons of Chinese ancestry had been born in China, they could not claim American citizenship on the basis of the Republican theory of birthright citizenship. Instead, as immigrants, their only conceivable route to citizenship was through the process of naturalization. This mechanism in turn was barred to the Chinese by the existing naturalization statute, which limited access to naturalization to "free white persons"—a limitation that had been inserted in the first naturalization act passed by Congress.[11]

While some Republicans argued that this racial classification was repugnant to basic principles of justice, others joined Democrats in continuing to insist that natives of Asia should be barred from citizenship. The treatment of the Burlingame Treaty of 1868 illustrates this point. The Burlingame Treaty not only declared that both China and the United States were in favor of the principle of free immigration but also provided that "Chinese subjects visiting or residing in the United States, shall enjoy the same privileges, immunities, and exemptions in respect to travel or residence, as may be enjoyed by the citizens or subjects of the most favored nation."[12]

Such clauses were fairly common in treaties between the United States and other nations.[13] However, in the debate over the ratification of the Burlingame Treaty, the language became controversial. A number of senators feared that the provision would override the existing naturalization law and require that Chinese immigrants be given the opportunity to become citizens. To avert this eventuality, the Senate added a clause—apparently unique—that stated that none of the provisions of the treaty required the United States to extend naturalized citizenship to Chinese immigrants. Though the Senate debates over ratification of the treaty took place in executive session and were therefore not recorded, the latter provision was apparently critical to the Sen-

---

11. 1 Stat. at Large 103 (1790).

12. *United States Statutes at Large*, vol. 16 (1868), p. 739.

13. *Congressional Globe*, 42d Cong., 2d sess., 910 (1872) (remarks of Sen. Nye).

ate's decision to ratify. Similarly, after brief but intense debates, in 1871 and 1872 many Senate Republicans joined Democrats to defeat efforts to remove the racial qualification from the naturalization laws, choosing instead to support a largely symbolic provision that specifically allowed natives of Africa to gain United States citizenship.[14]

After 1872, the political situation of the Chinese in America continued to deteriorate. In 1876, the platforms of both major political parties contained anti-Chinese planks; in the same year, a congressional committee was established to investigate the issues presented by Chinese immigration. While a minority of the committee members defended the Chinese and favored continued unfettered immigration, the majority report advocated the renegotiation of the Burlingame Treaty to permit the restriction of Chinese entry. A bill limiting the number of Chinese who could be carried by a single vessel to the United States passed both houses of Congress in 1878, only to be vetoed by President Rutherford B. Hayes on the ground that the limitation was inconsistent with existing treaty obligations.[15]

The legal obstacles to immigration restrictions were substantially reduced in 1880, when the Burlingame Treaty was renegotiated to allow the United States the option to "regulate, limit or suspend," but not "entirely prohibit," the entrance of Chinese la-

---

14. *Congressional Globe*, 42d Cong., 1st sess., 910 (1872); ibid., 41st Cong., 2d sess., at 4275–4276 (1870) (remarks of Rep. Sargent). Sargent's account was not questioned and is largely corroborated by 40th Cong., 3d sess., 1011 (1869) (remarks of Sen. Doolittle) and by ibid., 42d Cong., 2d sess., 910 (1872) (remarks of Sen. Nye).

15. *Republican Platform of 1876,* reprinted in Donald B. Johnson, comp., National Party Platforms, 1840–1956 (Urbana, Ill., 1978), 1:54 (calling for an investigation of problems created by Chinese immigration); *Democratic Platform of 1876*, reprinted in ibid., at 50 (calling for an end to Chinese immigration); "Views of the Late Oliver P. Morton on the Character, Extent, and Effect of Chinese Immigration to the United States," Sen. Misc. Doc. no. 20, 45th Cong., 2d sess. (1878); S. Rep. no. 689, 44th Cong., 2d sess. (1877); *Congressional Record*, 45th Cong., 3d sess., 1400, 1796 (1878).

borers. Two years later, a bill prohibiting the entrance of Chinese laborers for twenty years was adopted by both the House of Representatives and the Senate, only to meet once again with a presidential veto—this time by Chester A. Arthur. Soon thereafter, however, Arthur signed a ten-year moratorium into law. Subsequently, in 1888 the Geary Act extended the ban to include native Chinese who had come to the United States, departed, and later attempted to return.[16] Notwithstanding the fact that these statutes clearly violated even the renegotiated Burlingame Treaty, the Supreme Court upheld them against constitutional attack in *Chen Chae Ping v. United States*[17] and *Fong Yue Ting v. United States.*[18]

Because the immigration restrictions applied only to *federal* action, neither *Chen Chae Ping* nor *Fong Yue Ting* involved the interpretation of the Fourteenth Amendment. By contrast, the Citizenship Clause was directly implicated in *Wong Kim Ark v. United States*,[19] which came before the Supreme Court in 1898. Like *Elk*, *Wong Kim Ark* presented the Court with an issue not clearly resolved by the Fourteenth Amendment definition of citizenship. Wong Kim Ark was a man who had been born in the United States to Chinese parents. After visiting China, he was denied the right to reenter the United States by the Chinese Exclusion Act. He argued that the prohibitions of the Act did not apply to him because, having been born in the United States, he had become a citizen at birth and therefore could not be denied the right to reenter the country.

In purely doctrinal terms, *Wong Kim Ark* turned on the proper interpretation of the language of section 1 of the Fourteenth

---

16. James D. Richardson, *A Compilation of the Messages and Papers of the Presidents*, vol. 7 (New York, 1900), pp. 514–526; Sen. Exec. Doc. no. 148, 47th Cong., 1st sess. (1880); Richardson, *Compilation*, 8:112–118; 22 U.S. Stat. 88-61; 25 U.S. Stat. 504.

17. 130 U.S. 581 (1889).

18. 149 U.S. 698 (1893).

19. 169 U.S. 649 (1898).

Amendment, which provides that "[a]ll persons born...in the United States, and subject to the jurisdiction thereof" are citizens of the United States. Wong Kim Ark contended that this language embodied the common-law principle that birth within the territorial boundaries of a nation conferred citizenship in that nation. He argued simply that, as a person born in the United States, he was entitled to citizenship under the plain language of the amendment. This position was consistent with the legislative history of the Fourteenth Amendment; opponents of section 1 of the Fourteenth Amendment attacked language of the Citizenship Clause precisely because it would confer citizenship on such children, and at least one prominent Republican senator conceded the point.[20]

The counterargument focused on the requirement that the person born in the United States must also be "subject to the jurisdiction thereof." Relying on the Roman principle that a child's citizenship followed that of its parents, this argument rested on the contention that a child of Chinese parents born in the United States should be viewed as subject to the jurisdiction of the Chinese government, rather than that of the United States. *Dicta* in the 1873 decision in *The Slaughterhouse Cases* seemed to support this view.[21]

Of course, in the context of *Wong Kim Ark*, this argument had a clear racial subtext. The point emerged clearly in an *amicus* brief opposing Wong Kim Ark's claim:

> For the most persuasive reasons we have refused citizenship to Chinese subjects; and yet, as to their offspring, who are just as obnoxious, and to whom the same reasons for exclusion apply with equal force, we are told that we must accept them as fellow-citizens,

---

20. *Congressional Globe*, 39th Cong., 1st sess., 2939 (remarks of Sen. Hendricks), 2890 (remarks of Sen. Cowan), 2891 (remarks of Sen. Conness) (1866).

21. 83 U.S. (16 Wall.) 36 (1873).

> and that, too, because of the mere accident of birth. There certainly should be some honor and dignity in American citizenship that would be sacred from the foul and corrupting taint of a debasing alienage.[22]

Unmoved by this appeal to anti-Chinese prejudice, a divided Supreme Court concluded that Wong Kim Ark was in fact a citizen of the United States. Speaking for the majority, Justice Horace Gray essayed a detailed review of the common-law precedents dealing with the issue of birthright citizenship. After dismissing the language from *The Slaughterhouse Cases* as *dictum*, Gray observed that a contrary decision would threaten not only the claims of the descendants of the Chinese, but also the citizenship of descendants of immigrants from many other countries. In addition, however, Gray made a pointed reference to the impropriety of distorting legal principles in order to accommodate race-based legislation:

> Whatever considerations, in the absence of a controlling provision of the Constitution, might influence the legislative or the executive branch of the government to decline to admit persons of the Chinese race to the status of citizens of the United States, there are none that can constrain or permit the judiciary to refuse to give full effect to the peremptory and explicit language of the Fourteenth Amendment.[23]

Dissenting, Chief Justice Fuller took a different view of the import of the Citizenship Clause. Like Gray's majority opinion, Fuller's dissent focused primarily on the legal precedents on citizenship, ultimately concluding that they did not support Gray's position. However, Fuller ended his opinion by noting that what was at stake in *Wong Kim Ark* was congressional authority to

---

22. Quoted in Charles J. McClain, *In Search of Equality: The Chinese Struggle against Discrimination in Nineteenth-Century America* (Berkeley, 1996), p. 124.

23. *Wong Kim Ark*, 169 U.S. at 94.

make color-based distinction in citizenship determinations.[24] Thus, the influence of the race issue on his purportedly legal analysis was only thinly disguised.

Like *Elk*, *Wong Kim Ark* provides a clear example of a case in which the judicial interpretation of section 1 of the Fourteenth Amendment was dominated by distinctively legal principles. Moreover, in *Wong Kim Ark*, the Court must be credited with considerable courage for applying those principles in the face of appeals to widely shared ideals of racial superiority. However, despite its symbolic importance, the practical significance of the *Wong Kim Ark* decision was quite limited; under the regime established by the Chinese Exclusion Act, few people of Chinese parentage would in fact be eligible for citizenship by virtue of being born in the United States. By contrast, when faced with cases of greater practical import, the Court's decisions were more strongly influenced by ideological and political considerations.

---

24. Ibid., p. 732 (Fuller, C.J., dissenting).

Chapter 4

The Slaughterhouse Cases, Federalism, and Economic Regulation

As we have seen, those who drafted section 1 of the Fourteenth Amendment were concerned primarily with protecting the rights of free blacks and (to a lesser extent) Southern Unionists. However, the first case in which the Supreme Court was called upon to deal comprehensively with the scope of the rights protected by the Fourteenth Amendment did not involve either of these groups. Instead, it raised the claims of a relatively ordinary group of white people. These claims gave rise to *The Slaughterhouse Cases.*[1]

The factual background of *The Slaughterhouse Cases* can be described in relatively simple terms. In 1869, the legislature of the state of Louisiana had incorporated the Crescent City Stock Landing and Slaughter House Company and had granted the company the exclusive right to establish slaughterhouses and related businesses in the city of New Orleans and surrounding parishes. This monopoly was challenged by an organization of butchers who were effectively excluded from practicing their trade by the grant of the monopoly. The butchers made a variety of claims under both the Thirteenth and Fourteenth amend-

1. 83 U.S. (16 Wall.) 36 (1873). For differing viewpoints on *Slaughterhouse*, see Pamela Brandwein, *Reconstructing Reconstruction: The Supreme Court and the Production of Historical Truth* (Durham, N.C., 1999), and sources cited therein.

ments; however, their primary contention was that the grant of the monopoly violated the Privileges and Immunities Clause.

Slaughterhouse highlighted the major difficulty involved in the interpretation of the Privileges and Immunities Clause—the problem of defining the rights covered by the phrase "privileges or immunities of citizenship." Normally, one would have expected the seven Republicans on the Court to be more receptive to a broad reading of the Privileges and Immunities Clause, with its concomitant expansion of the role and authority of the federal government. In *Slaughterhouse* itself, however, other ideological and political imperatives complicated the debate. First, a government of carpetbaggers that was anathema to Democrats had adopted the state statute. Even more importantly, opposition to monopolies such as that granted to the Crescent City company had been a central tenet of Democratic ideology since the era of Andrew Jackson. Given these conflicting imperatives, it is not surprising that both the Democratic and Republican justices split in *Slaughterhouse*.

Four justices—Democrat Stephen Field and Republicans Salmon P. Chase, Joseph Bradley, and Noah Swayne—concluded that the Louisiana monopoly violated the Fourteenth Amendment. Field's opinion, which was also joined by Chase, Bradley and Swayne, was relatively narrow in scope. His analysis was based entirely on the view that the Fourteenth Amendment barred grants of "special and exclusive privileges" that deprived other citizens of "a right to pursue a lawful and necessary calling, previously enjoyed by every citizen." He argued that "what the [Comity Clause] does for the protection of citizens of one State against the creation of monopolies in favor of citizens of other States, the 14th Amendment does for the protection of every citizen of the United States against the creation of any monopoly whatever." Noting that monopolies such as that granted by the state of Louisiana were void at common law and had been held invalid by a number of state courts, Field declared that

> th[e] equality of right, with exemption from all disparaging and partial enactments, in the lawful pur-

> suits of life, throughout the whole country, is the distinguishing privilege of citizens of the United States. To them, everywhere, all pursuits, all professions, all avocations are open without other restrictions such as are imposed equally upon all others of the same age, sex and condition.

He concluded that "grants of exclusive privilege, such as is made by the Act in question, are opposed to the whole theory of free government."[2]

Although references to the Comity Clause figured prominently in his opinion, Field's analysis of the Fourteenth Amendment actually owed a greater debt to the antebellum state constitutional provisions prohibiting the grant of special privileges and immunities. His opinion thus drew on elements from both the Democratic and Republican approaches to postwar constitutionalism. On the one hand, Field's willingness to subject state legislation on local matters to significant federal oversight was a sharp departure from his Democratic roots and could only reflect the influence of Republican political thought. On the other hand, the antimonopoly theme of his argument embodied one of the central tenets of Jacksonian thought. In short, Field's approach was a kind of intellectual hybrid, owing substantial intellectual debts to both major political ideologies.

Bradley and Swayne, by contrast, each delivered opinions expounding a distinctively Republican theory of the Privileges and Immunities Clause. It was Bradley who provided the more detailed argument. He began by asking a much broader question than that addressed by Field: "Is it one of the rights and privileges of a citizen of the United States to pursue such civil employment as he may choose to adopt, subject to such reasonable regulations as may be prescribed by law?" Noting that the Fourteenth Amendment had established the primacy of national citizenship, Bradley traced the concept of privileges and immunities from the

2. *Slaughterhouse*, 83 U.S. 93, 88, 101, 111 (Field, J., dissenting).

Magna Carta through *Corfield v. Coryell*, concluding that "[no right] is more essential and fundamental than the right to follow such profession or employment as each one may choose, subject only to uniform regulations equally applicable to all." Bradley did concede that the Louisiana law could stand if it were a reasonable "police" regulation. However, noting the historic distaste for monopolies, he declared that the law "has none of the qualities of a police regulation" and was not reasonable, but rather was "onerous, unreasonable, arbitrary and unjust."[3] Thus, like Field, Bradley and Swayne had no difficulty in concluding that the grant of the monopoly violated the Fourteenth Amendment.

Bradley's reasoning, with its emphasis on the primacy of national citizenship and the rights appurtenant to such citizenship, echoed the arguments of those who had drafted both the Civil Rights Act of 1866 and the Fourteenth Amendment itself. Nonetheless, he and Field failed to convince a majority of the justices that the Louisiana law was invalid. When the case was initially argued in 1871, the Court split 4-4; on reargument in the next term, five justices voted to reject the constitutional challenge, with Democrat Nathan Clifford joining Republicans David Davis, Ward Hunt, Samuel Miller, and William Strong to form the majority.

Speaking for the majority, Miller characterized the Louisiana statute quite differently than did the dissenters. Rather than an odious effort to grant special privileges to a favored few, Miller saw a plausible (although admittedly debatable) attempt to deal with very real social problems. He asserted that

> it cannot be denied that the statute under consideration is aptly framed to remove from the more densely populated part of the city, the noxious slaughter-houses, and large and offensive collections of animals necessarily incident to the slaughtering business of a large city and to locate them where the convenience,

3. Ibid., pp. 112, 119 (Bradley, J., dissenting).

> health and comfort of the people require they shall be located. And it must be conceded that the means adopted by the Act for this purpose are appropriate, are stringent and effectual.[4]

The major difference between the majority and the dissenters, however, lay in their analysis of the Privileges and Immunities Clause itself.

Miller's argument began with a characterization of the Reconstruction amendments as primarily race-focused. He asserted that "the most cursory glance at these [amendments] discloses a unity of purpose, when taken in connection with the history of the times, which cannot fail to have an important bearing on any question of doubt concerning their true meaning," and that "no one can fail to be impressed with the one pervading purpose found in them all, lying at the foundation of each... we mean the freedom of the slave race, the security and firm establishment of that freedom, and the protection of the newly-made freeman and citizens from the oppressions of those who had formerly exercised unlimited dominion over him." While conceding that African Americans were not the only people who could claim the protections of the amendments, Miller contended that "in any fair and just construction of any section or phrase of these amendments, it is necessary to look to the purpose which we have said was the pervading spirit of them all."[5]

The majority opinion then turned specifically to the Privileges and Immunities Clause. Here the analysis began with a close reading of the specific language of the clause. Miller first noted that, on its face, the Fourteenth Amendment appeared to recognize two analytically separable classes of citizenship, declaring that persons born or naturalized in the United States are citizens both of the United States and of the state in which they reside. Next, he observed that, by its terms, the Privileges and Immuni-

4. Ibid., p. 64.
5. Ibid., pp. 67, 71.

ties Clause does not protect those rights derived from *state* citizenship, but only those appurtenant to the status of citizen of the United States. Miller argued, that even after the adoption of the Fourteenth Amendment, most rights remained incidents of state citizenship, and as such were subject to the protection and control of the state governments.[6] He defined the incidents of state citizenship by reference to the antebellum case-law interpreting the Comity Clause.

In particular, Miller focused on language from Justice Bushrod Washington's well-known circuit-court opinion in *Corfield v. Coryell*, which asserted that the rights protected by the Comity Clause "may . . . be comprehended under the following several heads: Protection by the government, with the right to acquire and possess property of every kind, and to pursue and obtain happiness and safety, subject, nevertheless, to such restraints as the government may prescribe for the general good of the whole." By contrast, Miller contended that only those rights that "owe their existence to the Federal government, its National character, its Constitution, or its laws" were entrusted to the care of the federal government by virtue of the Privileges and Immunities Clause.[7] Since in his view the right claimed in *Slaughterhouse* did not fit into any of these categories, Miller rejected the constitutional challenge.

Miller's argument in *Slaughterhouse* rested on three major premises: the idea that the Reconstruction amendments were designed primarily to protect the freed slaves, the distinction between national and state citizenship, and the thought that most rights remained exclusively associated with state citizenship. The second of these points is entirely unexceptionable; indeed, it was accepted by the dissenters as well as the majority. The remainder of Miller's analysis, however, faces serious difficulties.

First, his description of the Fourteenth Amendment as a mea-

---

6. Ibid., pp. 73–74, 74, 75–81.
7. Ibid., p. 79

sure designed to protect free blacks was at best only partially accurate. Admittedly, section 1 was aimed in large measure at the Black Codes, which had sharply curtailed the rights of freedmen in the former slave states. At the same time, however, John Bingham and other supporters of the Fourteenth Amendment also emphasized the need to provide federal protection for the rights of white Unionists in the states of the former confederacy. Thus, Bingham initially cited the Samuel Hoar affair, which involved a white man, as the prime example of the need for his amendment and later declared that his proposal would not only allow Congress to protect the freed slaves, but also would provide the authority "to protect the [many] loyal white citizens of the United States whose property, by State legislation, has been wrested from them by confiscation, and protect them from banishment." Moreover, in the final drafting process, the Joint Committee on Reconstruction rejected an explicit ban on racial discrimination with respect to civil rights in favor of the race-neutral language ultimately adopted.[8] Thus, Miller's characterization of the relationship between racial discrimination and the Fourteenth Amendment was substantially overstated.

His discussion of the significance of the Comity Clause cases is even more problematic. For Miller, the importance of *Corfield* and its progeny was that they recognized the centrality of the state governments in defining basic rights. In the actual congressional discussions of the Fourteenth Amendment, by contrast, these cases served a quite different function: Republicans consistently referred to the privileges and immunities discussed in *Corfield* and other cases as congruent with those that would be protected by the Privileges and Immunities Clause of the Fourteenth Amendment.[9] In short, Miller turned the significance of antebellum Comity Clause jurisprudence on its head.

8. *Congressional Globe*, 39th Cong., 1st sess., 158, 1065 (1866); Benjamin B. Kendrick, *The Journal of the Joint Committee on Reconstruction, 1865–1867* (New York, 1914), pp. 105–106.

9. See, for example, *Congressional Globe*, 39th Cong., 1st sess., 1835–1836, 2765 (1866).

Although *Slaughterhouse* by its terms dealt with *judicial* enforcement of fundamental rights, the decision also had clear implications for the scope of congressional power to adopt legislation implementing the Fourteenth Amendment. Indeed, the majority opinion in *Slaughterhouse* was clearly influenced by fears of undue centralization of legislative authority. In Miller's view, a narrow construction of the Privileges and Immunities Clause was necessary to preserve the basic structure of American federalism. He argued that Bradley's approach would "transfer the security and protection of all the civil rights . . . mentioned [in *Corfield*] from the States to the Federal Government," would "bring within the power of Congress the entire domain of civil rights heretofore belonging exclusively to the States," and would "constitute this court a perpetual censor upon all legislation of the States, on the civil rights of their own citizens, with authority to nullify such as it did not approve as consistent with those rights, as they existed at the time of the adoption of [the Fourteenth] Amendment." While conceding that under some circumstances he might be forced to accept such a result, Miller declared that

> when [the] consequences are so serious, so far reaching and pervading, so great a departure from the structure and spirit of our institutions; when the effect is to fetter and degrade the state governments by subjecting them to the control of Congress, in the exercise of powers heretofore universally conceded to them of the most ordinary and fundamental character; when in fact it radically changes the whole theory of the relations of the state and Federal Governments to each other and of both these governments to the people, the argument has a force that is irresistible, in the absence of language which expresses such a purpose too clearly to admit of doubt.[10]

Miller's emphasis on the importance of limiting the power of

10. *Slaughterhouse*, 83 U.S. 77–78.

Congress to enforce the Fourteenth Amendment implicitly reflected his fear of the potential interaction between the Privileges and Immunities Clause and the principles previously established by the Court in *Prigg v. Pennsylvania*[11] and *McCulloch v. Maryland*.[12] In *Prigg*, the Court was called upon to interpret the Fugitive Slave Clause, which provides that "[n]o Person held to Service or Labour in one State, under the Law thereof, escaping into another, shall, in Consequence of any Law or Regulation therein, be discharged from such Service or Labour, but shall be delivered up on Claim of the Party to whom such Service or Labour may be due." On its face, this provision seems only to prohibit state governments from emancipating fugitives by law and to impose a duty on states to return fugitive slaves. Moreover, the Constitution contains no specific authorization for Congress to enforce this clause. Nonetheless, in 1793, Congress adopted a statute that, among other things, criminalized private interference with the efforts of owners to retake fugitives.

In *Prigg*, the Court held that Congress had constitutional authority to adopt this provision. Speaking for the majority, Justice Joseph Story began the relevant portion of the opinion by observing that government aid would often be necessary for the claimant to recover the fugitive, and that the Clause itself, which provides that the slave "shall be delivered up, on claim of the [putative master]," seems to contemplate government enforcement.[13] Having concluded that the vindication of the constitutional guarantee required some government action, he then turned to the question of *which* government was charged with the duty of enforcement.

On this point, Story relied on the general principle that "where the end is required, the means are given; and where the duty is enjoined, the ability to perform it is contemplated to exist, on the part of the functionaries to whom it is entrusted."

---

11. 41 U.S. (16 Pet.) 539 (1842).
12. 17 U.S. (4 Wheat.) 316 (1819).
13. *Prigg*, 41 U.S. at 614–615.

Thus, Story argued, since the Fugitive Slave Clause was found in the federal Constitution, "the natural inference certainly is, that the national government is clothed with the appropriate authority and functions to enforce it." He scoffed at the contention that the lack of a specific enforcement provision was fatal to this contention, declaring, "If this be the true interpretation of the constitution, it must, in a great measure, fail to attain many of its avowed and positive objects, as a security of rights and recognition of duties," and noting that "[Congress] has, on various occasions, exercised powers which were necessary and proper as means to carry into effect rights expressly given, and duties expressly enjoined thereby." Thus, after reviewing in detail the specific provisions of the Fugitive Slave Act of 1793, he concluded that, with one narrow exception, the Act was "clearly constitutional, in all its leading provisions."[14]

Prigg seemingly established the proposition that Congress possessed inherent authority to legislate against private interference with rights that the Constitution protects against state infringement. Given the explicit grant of enforcement authority in section 5, the case for congressional power to protect Fourteenth Amendment rights from private interference was even stronger. This authority would have been particularly broad if linked with the language from *McCulloch*, where Chief Justice John Marshall stated: "Let the end be legitimate, let it be within the scope of the constitution, and all means which are appropriate, which are plainly adapted to that end, which are not prohibited, but consist with the letter and spirit of the constitution, are constitutional."[15] Thus, if the Privileges and Immunities Clause were deemed to cover the vast array of rights enumerated in *Corfield* and similar authorities, Congress would perforce have possessed authority to regulate a wide variety of private activity that had hitherto been under the exclusive control of the states. It was this regime that Miller refused to countenance in *Slaughterhouse*.

---

14. Ibid., pp. 615, 618–619, 622.
15. *McCulloch*, 17 U.S. at 421.

Commentators such as Laurence H. Tribe, Harold M. Hyman, and William M. Wiecek have contended that Miller's argument reflected an inability or unwillingness to accept the vision of federal relations that animated the framers of the Reconstruction amendments.[16] In fact, it closely paralleled the concerns of conservative Republicans such as Roscoe Conkling, Thomas T. Davis, Robert Hale, and William M. Stewart, whose fears regarding undue expansion of congressional authority led to the modification of the Fourteenth Amendment. Indeed, the language of the majority opinion in *Slaughterhouse* bears a striking similarity to Davis's attack on the early version of Bingham's amendment that was rejected precisely because it posed an undue threat to states' rights:

> Under [the language of this proposal] the constitutional functions of State Legislatures are impaired, and Congress may arrogate those powers of legislation which are the peculiar province of State organizations, and which cannot be taken from the States without a radical change in their relations. I will... consent to no centralization of power in Congress in derogation of constitutional limitations, nor will I lodge there today any grant of power which may... under the control of political aspirants or demagogues, be exercised in contravention of the rights and liberties of my countrymen.[17]

In the early 1870s, a number of prominent Republican legal commentators expressed similar concerns in arguing for a narrow interpretation of the Fourteenth Amendment.[18] Given this background, Miller's concerns must be viewed as consistent with at

16. Laurence H. Tribe, *American Constitutional Law* (Mineola, N.Y., 1982), pp. 551–552; Hyman and Wiecek, *Equal Justice under Law*, pp. 477–478.

17. *Congressional Globe*, 39th Cong., 1st sess., 1087 (1866).

18. James N. Pomeroy, "Political Precedents," *The Nation* 12 (1870): 300–301; Joseph Story, *Commentaries on the Constitution of the United States*, ed. Thomas M. Cooley (Boston, 1873), 2:683–685.

least one of the major themes of the Reconstruction-era debates over federalism.

Nonetheless, the dissenters were able to mount a powerful attack on the reasoning of the majority. Swayne confronted Miller's vision of post-Reconstruction federalism directly, arguing: "These [Reconstruction] Amendments are a new departure, and mark an important epoch in the constitutional history of the country. They trench directly upon the powers of the States, and deeply affect those bodies." Similarly, Bradley declared: "[I]t was the intention of the people of this country in adopting [the Fourteenth] Amendment to provide national security against violation by the States of the fundamental rights of citizens." At the same time, however, Bradley challenged Miller's apocalyptic vision of the practical consequences of a broad interpretation of the language of the amendment, suggesting that little congressional action would be needed to implement the amendment, and that after a brief period of adjustment, states would accommodate themselves to the new limitations, leaving few occasions for active federal intervention into state affairs. In any event, in Bradley's view, "[t]he great question is: what is the true construction of the Amendment?... The argument from inconvenience ought not to have a controlling influence in questions of this sort. The national will and national interest are of far greater importance."[19]

Swayne made the same argument even more pointedly. He first asserted that "no searching analysis of [section 1 of the Fourteenth Amendment] is necessary to eliminate [*sic*] its meaning. Its language is intelligible and direct.... Every word employed has an established significance. There is no room for construction. There is nothing to construe. Elaboration may obscure, but cannot make clearer the intent and purpose sought to be carried out." Then, responding specifically to Miller's effort to limit the scope

19. *Slaughterhouse*, 83 U.S. 125 (Swayne, J., dissenting), 123–124 (Bradley, J., dissenting).

of the amendment to racial discrimination, he declared, "[T]his Court has no authority to interpolate a limitation that is neither expressed nor implied. Our duty is to execute the law, not to make it."[20]

In purely formal terms, Swayne's argument was irrefutable. The drafters of the Fourteenth Amendment had used language with an established significance in antebellum jurisprudence, and the Court was bound to respect that established meaning in interpreting the amendment—even if some of the drafters themselves had not grasped the full import of their actions. Nonetheless, as Miller recognized, the approach of the dissenters posed very real dangers to the federal structure, dangers that had been envisioned by the moderate Republicans who had effectively controlled the drafting of the Fourteenth Amendment. When issues of congressional enforcement power were presented directly to the Court, these fears would shape even the views of the *Slaughterhouse* dissenters.

Among the enforcement cases, the 1876 decision in *United States v. Cruikshank*[21] provides the single most complete discussion of the constitutional theory underlying the Court's early interpretation of the Fourteenth Amendment. The case involved a challenge to a series of convictions obtained under section 6 of the Enforcement Act of 1870—the Pool amendment. The indictment on which the convictions were based charged that the defendants had entered into a conspiracy to deprive two citizens "of African descent and persons of color" of a number of rights. Some of the counts of the indictment were quite general, alleging that, because of the race of these citizens, the defendants had conspired to deprive them of the "free exercise and enjoyment of the rights, privileges, immunities and protections granted and secured to them... as citizens of the United States [and the] State of Louisiana" and "to hinder and prevent them... in their several

20. Ibid., pp. 126, 129 (Swayne, J., dissenting).
21. 92 U.S. (2 Otto) 542 (1876).

and respective free exercise and enjoyment of any right or privilege granted or secured to them by the constitution and laws of the United States." Speaking for a unanimous Court, Chief Justice Waite found these charges void as a matter of ordinary criminal procedure, concluding that they did not adequately specify *which* "privileges, rights and immunities" were the target of the defendant's allegedly illegal conspiracy.[22] Thus, in his treatment of these counts, Waite was not required to discuss the scope of congressional power to enforce the Reconstruction amendments.

The remaining counts of the indictment did not explicitly charge the defendants with discrimination on the basis of race. They did, however, allege that the defendants had conspired to deprive the named victims of specific rights. Some of the counts asserted that the victims had been hindered and prevented from exercising their right to vote; others cited the right to peaceably assemble and to keep and bear arms. Still others alleged a conspiracy to deprive the victims of their lives and liberty without due process of law. The voting rights allegations were dismissed on the authority of *United States v. Reese*,[23] which are discussed in the chapter 4. In dealing with the other counts, by contrast, the Court for the first time directly confronted the question of whether the Fourteenth Amendment incorporated the protections of the Bill of Rights.

Prior to the decision in *Cruikshank*, there seems to have been a widespread impression that the Privileges and Immunities Clause did indeed encompass the protections embodied in the first eight amendments.[24] Key Republicans such as Senator Jacob Howard of Michigan and Representative John A. Bingham of Ohio explicitly made this point during the consideration of the Fourteenth Amendment by the 39th Congress. Moreover, Democrats turned to the Bill of Rights as a device for limiting the scope of

---

22. Ibid., pp. 557–559.

23. Ibid., pp. 555–556.

24. The discussion that follows is taken from Earl M. Maltz, "The Concept of Incorporation," *University of Richmond Law Review* 30 (1999): 525–536.

the Privileges and Immunities Clause. Thus, for example, rejecting the claim that civil rights generally were associated with national citizenship, Democratic Senator Allen G. Thurman of Ohio argued,

> [By looking] to the provisions of the Constitution, we find what are the privileges and immunities of the people in their character as citizens of the United States. We find them by looking at the prohibitions contained in the Constitution against the infringement of certain rights, privileges and immunities which belong to the people and which, by these prohibitions, are recognized as rights which belong to a citizen of the United States, of which he cannot be deprived.

As examples, Thurman specifically mentioned the rights guaranteed by the first eight amendments.[25]

In addition, in *Slaughterhouse*, Justice Miller seemed to join dissenters Joseph P. Bradley and Noah Swayne in endorsing the concept of incorporation. Admittedly, the majority opinion in *Slaughterhouse* clearly gave the Privileges and Immunities Clause a very narrow reading. At the same time, however, while not explicitly referring to the Bill of Rights as a whole, Miller did cite "the right to peaceably assemble and petition for redress of grievances" as an example of a right of national citizenship protected by the Fourteenth Amendment.[26]

Viewed in isolation, the reference to the First Amendment right of assembly is most logically understood as supporting the doctrine of incorporation more generally. Miller described the privileges and immunities of national citizenship as those which "owe their existence to the Federal government, its national character, its Constitution, or its laws." The right of assembly is not

---

25. *Congressional Globe*, 39th Cong., 1st sess., 1089, 2765 (1866); 42d Cong., 2d sess., app. 25 (1872).

26. *Slaughterhouse*, 83 U.S. at 118, 79.

described as one that owes its existence to the federal government, but instead is linked to the privilege of *habeas corpus*, with both described as examples of "rights... guaranteed by the Federal Constitution." The most plausible implication is that the other rights that are explicitly guaranteed by the first eight amendments would be protected by the Fourteenth Amendment as well.[27]

This interpretation would also have fit comfortably with the context in which *Slaughterhouse* was decided. By any measure, Miller's interpretation of the Privileges and Immunities Clause was quite conservative; even if interpreted to incorporate the Bill of Rights, the majority opinion did no more than embrace the analysis of conservative Democrats during the Reconstruction era. However, any more limited view of his opinion would cast Miller as a reactionary whose view of the Fourteenth Amendment was more restricted than that of even the most conservative members of Congress. Such an interpretation is particularly unlikely, given the fact that Miller was a Republican, as were three of the remaining four members of his majority.

Moreover, even after the decision in *Slaughterhouse*, Democrats in Congress continued to assert that the Privileges and Immunities Clause was coextensive with the first eight amendments. Thus, in 1874, Senator Thomas M. Norwood of Georgia explicitly linked this view with *Slaughterhouse* itself, and Representative Roger Q. Mills of Texas also espoused the incorporation doctrine.[28] By contrast, no one seems to have suggested that Miller's opinion threatened the theory of incorporation.

Nonetheless, driven by their desire to protect the structure of federalism, all of the justices in *Cruikshank* rejected the concept of incorporation. Chief Justice Waite began his treatment of the issue with a reaffirmation of the *Slaughterhouse* distinction between the respective rights associated with state and national citi-

---

27. Ibid., p. 79.
28. 1 *Congressional Record*, app. 242, 383 (1874).

zenship. He then turned to a more general discussion of his view of the nature of American federalism, declaring that "the people of the United States resident within any State are subject to two governments: one State and the other National; but there need be no conflict between the two. The powers which one possesses, the other does not. They are established for different purposes, and have separate jurisdictions."[29] From a purely theoretical perspective, this vision of state/federal relations was hardly novel; indeed, it formed the basis of Joseph Story's approach to many areas of constitutional law, including the fugitive-slave question presented in *Prigg v. Pennsylvania*. In Story's hands, however, the theory of separate, exclusive spheres of authority was most often used as the basis for circumscribing the power of state governments. For Waite, by contrast, the theory became an instrument for restricting the scope of *federal* authority under section 5 of the Fourteenth Amendment.

The breadth of the exclusive authority of state governments was repeatedly emphasized in Waite's treatment of the provisions of the indictment that charged the defendants with incursions on interests protected by the Bill of Rights. His treatment of the Second Amendment right to keep and bear arms and the Fifth Amendment Due Process Clause are particularly significant. Waite argued that the right to keep and bear arms was neither created by the Second Amendment nor dependent upon the Constitution for its existence; instead, he contended, the Second Amendment simply forbade Congress from infringing upon a preexisting right. Thus, he concluded that citizens must look to their respective state governments for protection against the violation of the right by their fellow citizens.[30]

Waite viewed the counts charging the defendants with conspiring to deprive citizens of life and liberty without due process as "even more objectionable... nothing else than alleging a con-

29. *Cruikshank*, 92 U.S. at 550.
30. Ibid., p. 553.

spiracy to falsely imprison or murder citizens of the United States." While conceding that the rights to both life and liberty were natural rights, Waite declared, "The very highest duty of the States, when they entered into the Union under the Constitution[,] was to protect all persons within their boundaries in the enjoyment of these [rights]." Further, he stated, "Sovereignty, for this purpose, rests alone with the States." Based on this vision of federalism, Waite drew a sharp distinction between private action, which was left generally to state control, and state action, which the federal government could constitutionally control.[31]

To modern readers, one of the most striking aspects of both *Slaughterhouse* and *Cruikshank* is the Court's failure to make any reference to the legislative history of the Fourteenth Amendment. Subsequently, speaking for the majority in the 1900 decision in *Maxwell v. Dow*, Justice Rufus Peckham defended his refusal to consider Howard's explanation of the Privileges and Immunities Clause, declaring,

> It is clear that what is said in Congress on such an occasion may or may not express the views of the majority of those who favor the adoption of the measure which may be before that body, and the question of whether the proposed amendment itself expresses the meaning which those who spoke in its favor may have assumed it did, is one to be determined by the language actually therein used, and not by the speeches made regarding it. What individual Senators or Representatives may have urged in debate, in regard to the meaning to be given to a proposed constitutional amendment, or bill, or resolution, does not furnish a firm ground for its proper construction, nor is it important as explanatory upon which the members voted in adopting it. In the case of a constitutional amendment it is of less materiality than in that of an

31. Ibid.

> ordinary bill or resolution. A constitutional amendment must be agreed to, not only by Senators and Representatives, but it must be [by the states] before such amendment can take effect. The safe way is to read the language in connection with the known condition of affairs out of which the occasion for its adoption may have arisen, and then to construe it, if there be therein any doubtful expressions, in a way, so far as is reasonably possible, to forward the known purpose or object for which the amendment was adopted.[32]

Although Peckham's argument has been criticized by some modern commentators, his view was entirely consistent with the prevailing legal theories of the nineteenth century. During this period (with the notable exception of Harlan's dissent in *Elk v. Wilkins*), judges consistently asserted that courts should not rely on specific legislative history in construing statutes (and by extension, constitutional language). Instead, they simply considered the text of an enactment against the background of the context in which it was adopted.[33] Thus, given the existing legal culture, the failure of the Court to consider legislative history in *Slaughterhouse* and *Cruikshank* was entirely unexceptionable.

However, a strong case could be made for the incorporation doctrine, even without consulting the debates surrounding the adoption of the Fourteenth Amendment. As already noted, Bradley and Swayne had explicitly endorsed the doctrine in *Slaughterhouse*. Moreover, after he joined the Court in 1877, John Marshall Harlan became a persistent critic of the refusal to subject the states to the strictures of the Bill of Rights. Late in his

---

32. 176 U.S. 581, 601–602 (1900) (citations omitted).

33. Harlan's dissent in *Elk v. Wilkins*, 112 U.S. 94, 110–123 (1884), is a notable exception. Michael Kent Curtis (*No State Shall Abridge: The Fourteenth Amendment and the Bill of Rights* [Durham, N.C., 1986], p. 193) is one of the most prominent critics of the Court's methodology.

career, Stephen Field also adopted Harlan's position as his own.[34] Thus, the issue of incorporation remained highly controversial throughout the late nineteenth century.

In any event, the impact of the rejection of the concept of incorporation on judicial enforcement of constitutional rights can easily be overstated. To be sure, if the Court had accepted incorporation theory, it would have been substantially more sympathetic to the rights of criminal defendants in the late nineteenth and early twentieth centuries.[35] However, in most other areas, there is little indication that acceptance of the incorporation doctrine would have had a significant effect on the decisions of the Court.

First, the late-nineteenth-century Court showed little sympathy for claims based on the Free Speech and Free Exercise Clauses generally. In *In re Debs*,[36] the Court simply ignored what to modern eyes would seem to be a glaring free-speech issue. Similarly, in cases such as *Reynolds v. United States*,[37] *Davis v. Beason*,[38] and *Late Corporation of the Church of Jesus Christ of Latter-Day Saints v. United States*,[39] the Court gave an extremely narrow reading to the basic protections of the Free Exercise Clause. In such a jurisprudential atmosphere, the First Amendment would have been of little use to those challenging state government actions under any circumstances.

Conversely, neither the rejection of the incorporation doctrine nor Miller's narrow interpretation of the Privileges and Immunities Clause more generally had a lasting impact on the justices' willingness to deploy the Fourteenth Amendment to protect economic rights. Case law quickly demonstrated that the differences between the *Slaughterhouse* dissenters and the members of the

34. *O'Neil v. Vermont*, 144 U.S. 323, 338–339 (1892) (Field, J., dissenting).

35. See, for example, *Twining v. New Jersey*, 211 U.S. 208 (1908); *Hurtado v. California*, 110 U.S. 516 (1884).

36. 158 U.S. 564 (1895).

37. 98 U.S. (8 Otto) 145 (1878).

38. 133 U.S. 333 (1890).

39. 136 U.S. 1 (1890).

majority were less extreme than they first appeared. Moreover, the Court soon evinced an ability to protect economic rights without resort to the Privileges and Immunities Clause.

The first point emerged clearly in *Bartemeyer v. Iowa*[40] and *Bradwell v. Illinois*,[41] both of which were decided contemporaneously with *Slaughterhouse*. *Bartemeyer*, which was argued together with *Slaughterhouse*, was a challenge to an Iowa statute that barred the sale of "intoxicating liquors" in the state. The privileges and immunities aspect of the case presented little difficulty for the members of the *Slaughterhouse* majority; under the analysis that they had already adopted, the right to sell alcoholic beverages could not possibly be one of the privileges and immunities of national citizenship. Similarly, since *Bartemeyer* involved a challenge to a law of general applicability, rather than "class legislation," Field easily concluded that the case did not fall within the parameters established by his *Slaughterhouse* dissent.[42]

The remaining *Slaughterhouse* dissenters also agreed that the Iowa statute was constitutional. Given the breadth of Bradley and Swayne's dissents in *Slaughterhouse*, however, they believed that a more detailed explanation of their position in *Bartemeyer* was necessary. Thus, Bradley filed a concurrence that began by noting, "No one has ever doubted that a Legislature may prohibit the vending of articles deemed injurious to the safety of society, provided it does not interfere with the vested rights of property." He distinguished *Slaughterhouse* as a case in which the legislature had created a "noxious monopoly" that prevented most citizens from pursuing a "lawful avocation," and that the claim that the case presented a police regulation was a "mere pretext." By contrast, he characterized *Bartemeyer* as a case presenting "a claim of right to pursue an unlawful calling," which Bradley viewed as "occupying the same platform as a claim of right to disregard li-

40. 85 U.S. 129 (1873).

41. 83 U.S. 130 (1872).

42. *Bartemeyer*, 85 U.S. at 138 (Field, J., concurring).

cense laws and to usurp public franchises."[43] Viewed from this perspective, to hold the *Bartemeyer* statute unconstitutional would deprive the states of the ability to perform even standard government functions.

The Court's treatment of *Bradwell* fits comfortably with *Bartemeyer*. In *Bradwell*, the justices faced a problem that had greatly troubled conservative Republicans during the drafting of the Fourteenth Amendment—the possibility that section 1 would limit the ability of the states to make classifications based on gender. However, in 1866, Republican objections had focused primarily on the potential impact of the original equal protection language; no one seemed to recognize the possible implications of the Privileges and Immunities Clause for women's rights. Nonetheless, after the ratification of the amendment, feminist groups seized on this provision in an effort to advance their cause. The attempts of feminists to use the Fourteenth Amendment to secure the right to vote will be discussed in the next chapter; however, the claim in *Bradwell* was somewhat different. There, the issue was whether the state of Illinois could deny an otherwise qualified applicant the right to practice law solely on the ground that she was a woman. As in *Bartemeyer*, the members of the *Slaughterhouse* majority saw *Bradwell* as an easy case; since the Illinois rule did not involve racial discrimination and, in the view of the justices in the majority, the right to practice law was not an incident of federal citizenship, the question of whether women should be admitted to the bar remained solely in state hands.

Bradwell presented far more complex problems for Chase, Bradley, Field, and Swayne. They could not deny that Myra Bradwell was being denied the right to engage in generally lawful employment—a right that the *Slaughterhouse* dissenters had argued was protected by the Privileges and Immunities Clause. Moreover, the exclusion of women might well be characterized as the very sort of class legislation that Field had condemned so

---

43. Ibid., pp. 136–137 (Bradley, J., concurring).

strongly in his opinion. Thus, on its face, the logic of their position in *Slaughterhouse* might seem to require the four dissenters to accept Bradwell's argument.

Only Chase was willing to take this view, however. Speaking for himself, Field, and Swayne, Bradley relied on a natural-law argument to defend the action of the state of Illinois. Differentiating sharply between the privileges and immunities of men and women, he declared that

> the civil law, as well as nature herself, has always recognized a wide difference in the respective spheres and destinies of man and woman. . . . The constitution of the family organization, which is founded in the divine ordinance, as well as in the nature of things, indicates the domestic sphere as that which properly belongs to the domain and functions of womanhood. . . . The paramount destiny and mission of woman are to fulfill the noble and benign offices of wife and mother. This is the law of the Creator. . . .
>
> [I]t is within the province of the Legislature to ordain what offices, positions and callings shall be filled and discharged by men, and shall receive the benefit of those energies and responsibilities, and that decision and firmness which are presumed to predominate in the sterner sex.[44]

Bradley's opinions in *Bartemeyer* and *Bradwell* provide an indispensable counterpoint to his expansive argument in *Slaughterhouse*. Taken together, the two concurrences suggest that, in practical terms, the differences between the majority and the dissenters in *Slaughterhouse* were less dramatic than is sometimes suggested. To be sure, in purely doctrinal terms, all of the dissenters took a markedly different tack than the majority.

---

44. *Bradwell*, 83 U.S. at 141 (Bradley, J., concurring). In addition, see *In re Lockwood*, 154 U.S. 116 (1894) (rejecting a challenge to refusal to admit women to bar).

Nonetheless, in *Bartemeyer* and *Bradwell*, Bradley, Field, Swayne, and even Chase demonstrated that they were quite willing to leave the states with great latitude to make economic regulations.

Conversely, the majority's narrow reading of the Privileges and Immunities Clause did not deter the post-*Slaughterhouse* Court from deploying other provisions of the Fourteenth Amendment against economic regulations in some contexts. *Munn v. Illinois* provided an early indication of the Court's attitude. *Munn* was a challenge to an Illinois statute that fixed the amount that could be charged for the storage of grain in warehouses located in large metropolitan areas. The owners of a warehouse that had been constructed before the limitations were imposed challenged the statute, arguing that it violated the Due Process Clause of the Fourteenth Amendment. Over the dissents of Stephen Field and William Strong—the latter a member of the *Slaughterhouse* majority—in 1877 the Court rejected this and other constitutional challenges to the statute.[45]

Despite the similar conclusions in the two cases, the tenor of the majority opinion in *Munn* differed significantly from that in *Slaughterhouse*. First, as William E. Nelson has noted, both the majority and the dissent in *Munn* concluded that the Due Process Clause prohibited the legislature from interfering unduly with purely private contracts. Their only dispute was over the proper characterization of grain warehouses. Speaking for the majority, Chief Justice Morrison R. Waite analogized warehouses to such quasi-public entities as common carriers and innkeepers, whose businesses had historically been subject to extensive government regulation. Field, by contrast, argued that warehouses should be treated no differently than any other type of ordinary private property.[46]

45. 94 U.S. 113 (1877).

46. William E. Nelson, *The Fourteenth Amendment: From Political Principle to Judicial Doctrine* (Cambridge, Mass., 1988), pp. 171–174; *Munn*, 94 U.S. at 134, 139–140 (Field, J., dissenting).

Moreover, the central elements of the *Slaughterhouse* analysis are conspicuously absent from the *Munn* opinion. There is no discussion of the idea that the Reconstruction amendments were aimed primarily at racial discrimination; nor does Waite make any appeal to the concept of states' rights, which dominated Miller's opinion in *Slaughterhouse*. Instead, the majority and dissenting opinions each focused on the same two issues: the fundamental principles defining the relationship between the powers of government and the rights of citizens, and the proper interpretation of English, federal, and state authorities dealing with related issues.

This distinction reflects important differences between the Privileges and Immunities Clause and the Due Process Clause of the Fourteenth Amendment. As already noted, existing legal doctrine provided no clear principles that would have limited the scope of federal power under the Privileges and Immunities Clause; thus, Miller felt compelled to construct such principles in order to preserve the basic structure of American federalism. By contrast, the Court apparently had confidence that the general principles developed in the substantial antebellum jurisprudence dealing with due-process analysis provided at least a framework with which to fashion limitations on the reach of the same clause in the Fourteenth Amendment. These principles could be particularly significant in limiting congressional authority under the enforcement provisions of the Fourteenth Amendment—one of the major concerns of the *Slaughterhouse* majority. Thus, for example, in *Slaughterhouse* itself, the majority had been able to dispose of the due-process aspects of the constitutional challenge simply by noting the historical antecedents of the clause and asserting that "no construction of that provision that we have ever seen, or any that we deem admissible," would support the claim of the butchers.[47]

Nonetheless, the Waite Court was clearly aware that substan-

---

47. *Slaughterhouse*, 83 U.S. at 81–82.

tive due process analysis itself carried with it significant dangers, and was determined to craft principles that would reduce potential problems. *Davidson v. New Orleans*—decided the same year as *Munn*—provides a graphic illustration of their concern. *Davidson* was a due process challenge to the assessment of taxes on real estate in Louisiana. The Court unanimously rejected the challenge. Speaking for eight members of the Court, Miller began by noting the deep historical roots of the Due Process Clause, but conceded that "the phrase 'due process of law' remains today without that satisfactory precision of definition which judicial decisions have given to nearly all the other guarantees of personal rights found in the constitutions of the several States and of the United States." Miller saw "abundant evidence" that this lack of precision had created what he described as a "strange misconception" that "the clause...is...a means of bringing to [the Supreme Court] the abstract opinions of every unsuccessful litigant in a State court of the justice of the decision against him, and of the merits of the legislation on which such a decision may be founded." Miller argued that this misconception was best countered by the "gradual process of judicial inclusion and exclusion, as the cases presented for decision may require." In *Davidson*, over the objection of Joseph Bradley, the Court explicitly held that the substance of tax assessments could not be the subject of due process attack.[48] Nonetheless, the language of the opinion implicitly invited natural law and quasi-natural law arguments in later cases under the Fourteenth Amendment.

In 1886, these arguments found their first success in *Yick Wo v. Hopkins*. *Yick Wo* was a challenge to a San Francisco ordinance that required approval of the city Board of Supervisors to operate a laundry in a wooden building. Under the Court's interpretation of the ordinance, the Board of Supervisors had unfettered discretion to either grant or deny the application to operate such a laundry. While the supervisors had denied consent to each of the

48. 96 U.S. 96, 101–102, 104, 104–105 (1877).

two hundred Chinese who had applied for permission to operate laundries in wooden buildings, eighty non-Chinese had been granted such permission. Based on this view of the facts, a unanimous Court found the ordinance unconstitutional.[49]

While most modern commentators focus on the racial aspects of *Yick Wo*, race played little direct role in most of Justice Stanley Matthews's opinion for the Court. Instead, drawing on the antebellum legal principle that all persons were entitled to be judged by generalizable legal principles rather than by the whims of government officials, the opinion focused primarily on the arbitrary nature of the decision-making process. Matthews began by noting that, while not citizens, the Chinese immigrants could claim the benefit of both the Burlingame Treaty and the Due Process and Equal Protection clauses of the Fourteenth Amendment, and that the Civil Rights Act of 1870 had reaffirmed this protection. Matthews then emphasized that what was at stake in *Yick Wo* was an aspect of "the fundamental rights to life, liberty and property" and declared that "the very idea that one man may be compelled to hold his life, or the means of living, or any material right essential to the enjoyment of life, at the mere will of another, seems to be intolerable in any country where freedom prevails, as being the essence of slavery itself." In characterizing the *Yick Wo* ordinance as imposing just such a requirement, the Court analogized the situation to cases involving the arbitrary fixing of utility rates and the forced removal of a steam engine from a box-maker's shop. Thus, the Court suggested that the ordinance was unconstitutional on its face.[50]

Yick Wo is the earliest example of the Court's invocation of the Fourteenth Amendment against what it viewed as an arbitrary exercise of state power to control the economy. While the case itself focused only on the arbitrariness of the procedure involved, the

---

49. 118 U.S. 356, 374 (1886). The facts of the case may not in fact have so clearly reflected discrimination against the Chinese. Laurence H. Tribe, *American Constitutional Law*, p. 1483 n. 3.

50. *Yick Wo*, 118 U.S. at 368–369, 370, 371, 372, 373.

clear implication of the analysis (particularly when paired with the *Munn* opinion) is that the Fourteenth Amendment would be a barrier to arbitrary substantive action as well. This implication was affirmed in 1897 in *Chicago, B & Q.R. Co. v. City of Chicago*. There, speaking for the Court, in language that echoed the pre-war decisions in *Wynnhamer v. New York*[51] and *Hoke v. Henderson*,[52] Harlan declared,

> Due process of law, as applied to judicial proceedings instituted for the taking of private property for public use means... such process as recognizes the right of the owner to be compensated if his property be wrested from him and transferred to the public. The mere form of the proceeding against the owner, even if he be admitted to defend, cannot convert the process into due process of law, if the necessary result be to deprive him of his property without compensation.[53]

Chicago, B. & Q.R. Co. is the first example of the use of the Due Process Clause to subject the states to one of the substantive principles of the Bill of Rights—in that case, the Just Compensation Clause of the Fifth Amendment. Together with decisions such as *Munn* and *Yick Wo*, it clearly presaged a determination to provide judicial protection for rights closely related to those for which the Court had apparently shown little enthusiasm in *Slaughterhouse*. Combined with the doctrine of federal-state relations outlined in *Cruikshank*, the cases also reflect a commitment to conservative legal principles. Analogous principles informed the Court's treatment of political rights as well; however, they were to some degree counterbalanced by a distaste for classifications explicitly designed to discriminate against the newly freed slaves.

---

51. 15 N.Y. 378 (1856).
52. 15 N.C. (4 Dev.) 1 (1833).
53. 166 U.S. 226, 236–237 (1897).

Chapter 5

The Reconstruction Amendments and Political Rights

The late nineteenth century saw an intense debate over the relationship of the Reconstruction amendments to political rights. During the drafting process, the issue of voting rights was extensively discussed. Thus, it is not surprising that the Supreme Court was called upon to adjudicate the impact of the amendments on the right to vote. In addition, however, the Court faced a variety of issues related to another political right that received less attention during the congressional debates—the right to serve on juries.

Even as early as 1866, most Republican members of Congress wished to eliminate racial qualifications for suffrage. Indeed, at one point the Joint Committee on Reconstruction voted to report a constitutional amendment that would have prohibited the states from imposing such qualifications after the year 1876. However, it soon became clear that this proposal was a political liability, and the vote was quickly reversed. During the debates over the language that was ultimately reported, both Jacob Howard and John A. Bingham vigorously denied Democratic charges that the Privileges and Immunities Clause would enfranchise the freed slaves. This conclusion was echoed (sometimes with regret) by other prominent Republicans as well.[1]

---

1. *Congressional Globe*, 39th Cong., 1st sess., 2508, 2542, 2766 (1866); *Report of the Joint Committee on Reconstruction*, 39th Cong., 1st sess., 12 (1866).

Republicans were on solid legal ground in making their claims on this point. Despite contrary *dicta* in the Circuit Court opinion in *Corfield v. Coryell*, the right to vote could not have been protected by the Comity Clause. Otherwise, states would have been required to grant mere sojourners from other states the right to vote in elections—a possibility that no one appears to have seriously entertained in the antebellum era. Since the Privileges and Immunities Clause of section 1 was drawn directly from the Comity Clause, it seems logical to conclude that the right to vote was also outside the purview of the Fourteenth Amendment.

The failure to protect voting rights in the Fourteenth Amendment did not end the discussion, however. By 1869, Republicans were united in their determination to pass a constitutional amendment that addressed the suffrage issue directly. The congressional debates that followed were much more extensive and complex than those that culminated in the passage of the Fourteenth Amendment. Like the debates of 1866, to a certain degree they reflected the fact that the Fifteenth Amendment was in part a political statement. However, the debates reflected even more clearly an awareness that the amendment would create new law, and that the import of that law would be determined by distinctively legal principles.[2]

This point is illustrated by the reactions of Republicans of all stripes to the language that was ultimately adopted. Advocates of truly universal manhood suffrage pointed out that simply to prohibit race discrimination would leave the states free to adopt a variety of restrictions that, although neutral on their face, would, in the words of Republican Senator Frederick A. Sawyer of South Carolina, "practically disfranchise four-fifths of the citizens of African descent." Opponents of broader language did not dispute this characterization. Instead, they were willing to accept this re-

---

2. These debates are recounted in William Gillette, *The Right to Vote: Politics and the Passage of the Fifteenth Amendment* (Baltimore, 1965); Maltz, *Civil Rights*, ch. 9; and Xi Wang, *The Trial of Democracy: Black Suffrage and Northern Republicans* (Athens, Ga., 1997).

sult in order to avoid intruding unduly on state prerogatives and endangering the ultimate ratification of the amendment.[3] It was against this background that the Supreme Court faced a variety of suffrage-related issues in the late nineteenth century.

The Court's first encounter with the suffrage issue involved efforts by women to obtain the right to vote. Some late-nineteenth-century feminists contended that under the newly ratified Fourteenth Amendment, Congress possessed the authority to enfranchise them by statute.

Although it drew support from some radical Republicans, this position was emphatically rejected by majorities in the Judiciary Committees of both houses of Congress. The House Judiciary report was prepared by Republican Representative John A. Bingham of Ohio, the author of section 1 of the Fourteenth Amendment, while the Senate report was the work of Republican Senator Matthew W. Carpenter of Wisconsin. Both reports focused on issues of federalism. They first noted that the original Constitution had left the matter of qualifications for voting entirely with the states. Turning to the impact of the Fourteenth Amendment, both Bingham and Carpenter argued that section 2 of the amendment implicitly recognized the continued authority of the states over voter qualifications. They agreed that the right to vote was not one of the "privileges and immunities of citizenship" guaranteed by section 1 of the amendment—a view that Bingham had also expressed during the debates over the adoption of the Fourteenth Amendment in 1866. Thus, both reports concluded that Congress had no authority to legislate on the subject beyond that provided by section 2 of the Fifteenth Amendment, which dealt with racial discrimination only.[4]

---

3. *Congressional Globe*, 40th Cong., 3d sess., 1010, 1009, app. 97–99 (1869).

4. H. R. Rep. no. 22, 41st Cong., 1st sess., 2, 3, 1-2 (1871); S. Rep. no. 21, 42d Cong., 2d sess., 1, 3, 3-4 (1872). Ironically, the following year Carpenter was counsel for Myra Bradwell in *Bradwell v. Illinois*, 83 U.S. (16 Wall.) 130 (1873), discussed above.

Similarly, in 1874, the Supreme Court unanimously rejected the feminist arguments in *Minor v. Happersett.* Speaking for the Court in that case, Chief Justice Morrison R. Waite relied on both textual and historical arguments to support his position. Waite conceded that the status of citizenship itself had not been limited to men. At the same time, however, he also observed that, if the right to vote were one of the privileges and immunities of citizenship, nonresident transients could claim the right to vote under the Comity Clause; that section 2 of the Fourteenth Amendment allowed states to limit the suffrage to men without penalty; and that the Fifteenth Amendment would have been considered unnecessary if the Reconstruction Congresses had believed the right to vote to be covered by the guarantees of the Fourteenth Amendment. Waite also noted that suffrage had historically been limited to males and that state governments had nonetheless been considered "republican in form" when the Constitution was drafted. Thus, he concluded that "if the courts can consider any question settled, this is one. For nearly ninety years the people have acted upon the idea that the Constitution, when it conferred citizenship, did not necessarily confer the right to suffrage... the Constitution does not confer the right of suffrage upon anyone."[5] This conclusion would have profound implications when, two years later, the Court considered the constitutionality of the Enforcement Act of 1870 in *United States v. Reese.*[6]

Reese arose from an indictment that was based on sections 3 and 4 of the Enforcement Act of 1870. The indictment charged that the defendants had failed, "on account of... race and color," to allow an African American to pay the capitation tax that was a prerequisite to voting and had also refused to receive the vote of the African American after being presented an affidavit confirming his willingness to pay the tax. With only one dissent, the

5. 88 U.S. 162 (1874).
6. 92 U.S. 214 (1876).

Court quashed the indictment. Speaking for seven justices, Chief Justice Waite gave the relevant sections of the statute an unusually broad interpretation, holding that they were not limited to discrimination based on race or color, but rather prohibited all wrongful refusals to allow a person to qualify to vote. Waite concluded that, thus construed, these sections of the statute went well beyond the power granted to Congress by the Fifteenth Amendment and as such could not form the basis of a valid indictment.[7]

As the concurrence of Democrat Nathan Clifford and the dissent of Republican Ward Hunt amply demonstrate, Waite's reading of the Enforcement Act was questionable at best. Nonetheless, from a constitutional perspective, the limitations that the *Reese* Court imposed on the power of Congress were far from novel.[8] Indeed, they amounted to nothing more than a reaffirmation of the principles of *Minor v. Happersett*—principles that, as we have seen, were accepted by many mainstream Republicans during the Reconstruction era and were entirely consistent with the conclusions mandated by the principles of ordinary legal analysis. Conversely, when in 1884 those same principles suggested a more expansive reading of congressional power in *Ex Parte Yarbrough*,[9] the Waite Court also proved willing to accept their implications.

Like *Reese, Yarbrough* arose from an indictment that alleged

---

7. Ibid., pp. 217–220.

8. Ibid., pp. 225–227 (Clifford, J., concurring), 241–245 (Hunt, J., dissenting).

The decision to adopt the broad reading may have represented a tactical retreat in the face of a change in the political climate. Dissatisfaction with the course of Reconstruction had been a significant factor in the Republican electoral reverses in 1874. A decision directly upholding the Enforcement Act could have added fuel to charges that Republicans were bent on indefinitely continuing supervision over the Southern electoral process. At the same time, the 1874 defeat made it unlikely that aggressive enforcement action would continue in any event. By adopting the broad reading, the Court avoided the political consequences of upholding the prosecution while preserving the possibility that a future Congress could intervene on behalf of black voters if political circumstances changed.

9. 110 U.S. 651 (1884).

that a number of private parties had conspired to interfere with the free exercise of suffrage by an African American citizen in violation of the Enforcement Act of 1870. The indictment in *Yarbrough*, however, differed in one critical respect from that in *Reese*: it specifically alleged that the interference was intended to prevent the citizen from voting in *federal* elections—elections protected separately by the Enforcement Act. This difference proved crucial to the decision. Speaking for a unanimous Court, Justice Miller declared, "If this government is anything more than a mere aggregation of delegated agents of other States and governments, each of which is superior to the general government [the essence of the state sovereignty heresy], it must have the power to protect the elections on which its existence depends from violence and corruption." Analogizing the Enforcement Act to statutes protecting federal officers in the performance of their duties, Miller declared, "The [constitutional] power in either case arises out of the circumstance that the function in which the party [protected] is engaged or the right which he is about to exercise is dependent on the laws of the United States." He rejected the argument that the right to vote for federal office was simply a function of state law, asserting that Article I, section 2, simply adopts state-law standards "as the qualification of its own electors for members of Congress."[10]

Even if Miller had said no more in *Yarbrough*, the case would have armed Congress with substantial power to protect blacks from private efforts to prevent them from voting. After all, in most cases, those who would attempt to prevent blacks from registering would be making no distinction between registration to vote in state and federal elections. Moreover, in many instances state and federal elections are held simultaneously, and an effort to prevent a person from voting in one would necessarily be an effort to prevent the same person from voting in both. Thus, by focusing on the federal element, the federal government could

10. Ibid., pp. 657, 662, 663.

constitutionally reach a wide variety of private interference with the state electoral process as well. Miller, however, went further, seemingly making a conscious decision to suggest that the Fifteenth Amendment provided Congress with authority to prevent private, racially motivated interference with the right to vote generally. Distinguishing *Reese*, Miller first analogized the right to vote in federal elections to the Fifteenth Amendment right to be free from racial discrimination in voting rights. He then declared that "the exercise of the right in both instances is guaranteed by the Constitution, and should be kept free and pure by congressional enactments whenever that is necessary."[11] Thus, he implicitly accepted the proposition that the Fifteenth Amendment armed Congress with the authority to prevent private action that denied people the right to vote on the basis of race.

Miller was clearly aware of the apparent dissonance between the *Yarbrough* analysis and the formalistic definition of rights that had figured so prominently in *The Civil Rights Cases*,[12] decided only a year before. Distinguishing the Fourteenth Amendment state action cases, he asserted that

> while it may be true that acts which are mere invasions of private rights, which acts have no sanction in the statutes of a State, or which are not committed by any one exercising its authority, are not within the scope of that amendment, it is quite a different matter when Congress undertakes to protect the citizen in the exercise of rights conferred by the Constitution of the United States essential to the healthy organization of the government itself.[13]

At first glance, the *Yarbrough* decision might seem to reflect a vision of federalism that diverges sharply from the earlier cases, which severely circumscribed congressional power to enforce the

---

11. Ibid., p. 664.
12. 109 U.S. 3 (1883).
13. *Yarbrough*, 110 U.S. at 666.

Reconstruction amendments. In many respects, however, the parallels between Miller's *Yarbrough* analysis and the approach of the *Cruikshank* Court are striking. Both opinions posit a set of preexisting rights whose protection is remitted to the state governments. At the same time, Congress is viewed as having plenary power to enforce rights whose very existence is derived from the Constitution. Thus, rather than representing a sharp departure from existing doctrine, *Yarbrough* can be viewed as presenting the flip side of that doctrine.

Taken as a whole, the Waite Court's elaboration of the constitutional standards governing voting rights cases reflects a perfectly plausible application of the principles of ordinary legal analysis. Relying on the well-established distinction between civil rights and political rights, the Court followed the principles established during the antebellum era and held that the language of section 1 had no impact on the political right of voting. However, during this era, the Court also was called upon to consider the impact of the Fourteenth Amendment on another important political right—the right to serve on a jury. In dealing with the jury service cases, the Court expanded the scope of the Fourteenth Amendment beyond that either envisioned by the drafters or required by the principles of ordinary legal analysis.

Students of the Reconstruction amendments have paid relatively little attention to the issue of racial discrimination in the selection of jurors.[14] In some respects, this lack of emphasis is entirely understandable. During the Reconstruction era, the ability to serve on a jury was viewed as a species of political right, and the struggle over political rights in the late nineteenth century fo-

14. Notable exceptions include Akhil Reed Amar, *The Bill of Rights: Creation and Reconstruction* (New Haven, 1998); Vikram D. Amar, "Jury Service as Political Participation Akin to Voting," *Cornell Law Review* 80 (1995): 203–259; and Benno C. Schmidt, "Juries, Jurisdiction and Race Discrimination: The Lost Promise of *Strauder v. West Virginia*," *Texas Law Review* 61 (1983): 1401–1499.

cused primarily on the right to vote. At the same time, however, jury selection was also understood to have an independent significance; moreover, it was a jury discrimination case that would produce the Supreme Court's most powerful indictment of state-imposed racial discrimination in the post-Reconstruction era.

The parallels between jury service and suffrage were clearly reflected in 1864 during the debate over Republican efforts to allow African Americans to appear as witnesses in all cases in federal court. Opposing these efforts, Democratic Senator Thomas A. Hendricks of Indiana complained that "if it is right to bring [African Americans] into court to testify in a case between white men... why not place him in the jury box, and let him decide what shall be the verdict in the case between two white men." Analogizing the position of African Americans to that of children and women, Republican Senator James Harlan of Iowa responded,

> The truth is they depend upon entirely different considerations. The child may at a very early period be capable of telling the truth... of stating facts that come under his observation, yet incapable to adjudicate a question of law or a question of fact. So [it is] in relation to the correlative rights to vote and hold office.... These rights are not natural rights; they are rights that arise under the law by the common consent of the whole.... The right to vote, to hold office, to aid in making the laws, in adjudicating and enforcing them, is derived from the civil society of which the parties are members.[15]

Indeed, allowing African Americans to sit on juries was, if anything, even more controversial than granting them the right to vote. Although African Americans could vote in five Northern

15. *Congressional Globe*, 38th Cong., 1st sess., 839, 840 (1864).

states prior to the Civil War, only the state of Massachusetts admitted them to the jury box.[16] One reason for the distinction is that allowing African Americans the right to vote simply provided them the opportunity to participate in the choice of government officials, while jury service allowed them to make government decisions themselves—at times, in effect, to rule white people. In 1867, Democratic Senator Reverdy Johnson of Maryland made this point in opposing legislation designed to admit African Americans to jury service in the District of Columbia:

> The objections to [this] measure . . . are much stronger than those which were applicable to the . . . question of granting them the right to suffrage. From the consequences of the exercise of that right there is comparatively . . . little to be apprehended. The large numerical majority of white people in the United States is perhaps a security against any serious disadvantage that might happen to the country at large. But this is not the case as far as concerns [jury service]. . . . The question for the Senate to decide is whether we are willing to have ourselves tried by a jury of black men for the most part just removed from slavery, without the capacity absolutely necessary to a faithful and intelligent discharge of that duty . . . thus our citizens and ourselves may be subjected to a judgment over which there is no revising power . . . pronounced by twelve ignorant black men.[17]

Against this background, it should not be surprising that even Republicans in Congress were initially unwilling to take action

16. Leon F. Litwack, *North of Slavery: The Negro in the Free States, 1790–1860* (Chicago, 1961), and Paul Finkelman, "Prelude to the Fourteenth Amendment: Black Legal Rights in the Antebellum North," *Rutgers Law Journal* 17 (1986): 415–443, survey the legal position of African Americans in the free states prior to the Civil War.

17. *Congressional Globe*, 40th Cong., 2d sess., 39 (1867).

guaranteeing the right of African Americans to serve on juries. Indeed, the distinction between civil and political rights generally was central to the construction of the Civil Rights Act of 1866 and section 1 of the Fourteenth Amendment. Democrats at times complained that both measures were designed to grant African Americans the right to vote and to sit on juries. However, mainstream Republicans almost uniformly took the view expressed by Representative James F. Wilson of Iowa, the floor manager of the Civil Rights Act, who denied that the language of the Act "confers [the right to serve on juries] upon the emancipated people, nor any portion of the people of the United States, who are not under the laws of the several States qualified to act as jurors." Similarly, as already noted, while the issue of jury service was not specifically addressed, Republicans repeatedly stressed that the language of the Fourteenth Amendment did not provide African Americans with political rights.[18]

As the Reconstruction era progressed, Republicans showed an increasing willingness to take measures that would protect the political rights of African Americans. The first such measure was limited to the District of Columbia. In early 1867, Congress overrode President Andrew Johnson's veto and granted African Americans the right to vote in the District.[19] However, efforts to take similar action with respect to jury service initially encountered frustrating procedural obstacles.

A bill allowing African Americans to serve on juries in the District of Columbia was first passed by veto-proof majorities in mid-1867. Nonetheless, because the bill did not arrive on his desk until the very end of the first session of the 40th Congress, President Johnson was able to kill the initiative by simply refusing to sign it. Republicans tried again in the second session of the

18. See, for example, ibid., 39th Cong., 1st sess., 2538 (1866) (remarks of Rep. Rogers); ibid., app. 157, pp. 632, 1832, 25, 2542, 2766. A notable exception to the opinion held generally by mainstream Republicans can be found at ibid., app. 157 (remarks of Rep. Delano).

19. Ibid., 39th Cong., 2d sess., 313, 344 (1867).

40th Congress in late 1867; this time, however, Johnson received the bill during the Christmas recess, and he once again claimed the right to exercise a pocket veto. While Republicans protested that a pocket veto was ineffectual in this context, for all practical purposes Johnson had once again prevailed.[20] Republicans were ultimately successful in passing the District of Columbia bill into law only after the election of 1868 brought Ulysses S. Grant to the presidency.

Even after the election of Grant, however, attempts to take action with a nationwide scope encountered formidable ideological and political problems. Foremost among these were issues related to federalism. Congressional authority over the District of Columbia was plenary; by contrast, federal regulation of conduct in the states is constitutionally acceptable only if authorized by one of the powers of Congress enumerated in the Constitution. Further, during the Reconstruction era, even constitutionally permissible actions by the federal government were viewed with suspicion if they infringed upon what were viewed as the legitimate prerogatives of the states. Of course, such concerns did not prevent Republicans from addressing the right to vote through the Fifteenth Amendment. By contrast, no such amendment specifically dealt with the question of service on juries. Nonetheless, jury service emerged as a hotly contested issue during the evolution of what was to become the Civil Rights Act of 1875.

Although the Act was not ultimately adopted until after his death, Senator Charles Sumner of Massachusetts was the driving force behind this statute. Throughout his political career, Sumner was an uncompromising opponent of racial discrimination in all of its forms. Moreover, he cared little for the concept of federalism, declaring that "*anything for Human Rights is constitutional*" and that "there can be no State Rights against Human Rights."[21]

---

20. *Congressional Globe*, 40th Cong., 1st sess., 677, 725, 726 (1867); 40th Cong., 2d sess., 51, 98, 720–721 (1867–68).

21. Ibid., 40th Cong., 1st sess., 902 (1867) (emphasis in original). The classic study of Sumner's life and ideology is David Donald's two-volume biogra-

Beginning in 1869, Sumner repeatedly introduced bills that not only would have barred racial discrimination in the selection of jurors, but also would have outlawed racial segregation by the public schools, common carriers, innkeepers, owners of theaters, and churches. Because of its breadth, Sumner's bill tested the limits of federal power to attack racial discrimination.

Sumner's measure did not reach the Senate floor until 1871, when it was proposed as an amendment to the Amnesty Bill of 1871. While the supporters of Sumner's proposal were successful in appending it to the Amnesty Bill, the addition of the civil rights provision proved fatal to the bill itself. The proponents of the civil rights measure continued to press their cause in each subsequent legislative session. They finally achieved a measure of success in 1875, as the lame-duck second session of the 43d Congress enacted a new Civil Rights Act into law. However, the statute that was adopted fell far short of Sumner's original proposal: the provisions dealing with schools, churches, and cemeteries were jettisoned, leaving only the sections dealing with common carriers, juries, inns, and places of amusement.

The jury service provision was included despite constant attacks on its constitutionality by not only Democrats, but also a number of mainstream Republicans. For example, although he defended the constitutionality of a number of the provisions of Sumner's bill, Senator Matthew H. Carpenter of Wisconsin led the Republican opposition to federal regulation of jury selection. Distinguishing sharply between the right to testify and the right to serve on a jury, Carpenter argued that

> Congress has no more power to determine the qualification of a juror in a State court, than it has to determine the qualification of a judge for the bench of a State court.... [A] distinction...exists between those

phy, *Charles Sumner and the Coming of the Civil War* (New York, 1960) and *Charles Sumner and the Rights of Man* (New York, 1970).

> privileges which are incident to American citizenship, which no State under the fourteenth amendment may abridge, and those political rights or franchises which a State, even since the fourteenth amendment, may grant or deny to its citizens at pleasure.[22]

Carpenter's argument echoed the apparent understanding of those who drafted the Fourteenth Amendment in 1866; however, by the 1870s, a change in perception of the situation drove most Republicans to look more favorably upon the jury service provision. Initially, they believed that the freed slaves would be adequately protected by federal guarantees of their civil rights. However, it soon became clear that, unless the federal government was willing to maintain an ongoing, massive presence in the South, guarantees of civil rights for African Americans would effectively be useless without access to the institutions of political power. While the adoption of the Fifteenth Amendment focused only on the issue of black suffrage, Republicans also understood that African Americans were too often victims of a biased judicial process. Thus, in 1868, it was reported that in many areas, the all-white juries of the South "still carry out the doctrine that 'the negro has no rights which the white man is bound to respect.'"[23]

Some Republicans also viewed the institution of the all-white jury as an important factor in the wider struggle for political control of the South. They reasoned that since whites in most Southern states were Democrats, an African American might be reluctant to espouse the Republican cause for fear that he might someday be forced to confront a jury that would hold his political allegiance against him. Republican Representative William J. Purman of Florida made this point clearly in urging support for the jury service provision:

> Every colored man suing for his wages brings his case before a jury who are prejudiced against him because

22. *Congressional Globe*, 42d Cong., 1st sess., 827 (1872).
23. H. R. Rep. No. 30, 40th Cong., 2d sess., 29 (1868).

> of his color. Every colored man tried as a criminal appears before a jury who are inclined to believe him guilty because of this race, and in both cases the fear of an adverse judgment may be held over him to force him to vote with [the Democratic] party which has been his implacable foe.[24]

However compelling these arguments might have been in a political sense, they were not alone sufficient to answer the constitutional challenge of Carpenter and his allies. Despite the fact that the Fifteenth Amendment dealt with political rights, it was of little use to Sumner and his allies. During the protracted discussions of the amendment, one of the most hotly contested issues was whether the change in the Constitution should deal with the right to hold political office as well as the right to vote. If race-blind access to political office had in fact been guaranteed by the Fifteenth Amendment, one might plausibly have taken the view that the amendment was understood to protect political rights generally, and as such guaranteed African Americans a right to be considered for jury service. However, the conference committee made a conscious decision to exclude office-holding from the final draft of the amendment. As Republican Senator Henry Wilson of Massachusetts observed with dismay, this omission obviated any possible inference that the amendment covered jury service—a point that Carpenter would later make explicitly in the debate over the Civil Rights Act.[25]

---

24. *Congressional Globe*, 43d Cong., 1st sess., 427 (1874).

25. Ibid., 40th Cong., 3d sess., 1296 (1869); ibid., 42d Cong., 1st sess., 827 (1872).

Vikram D. Amar suggests that the reason for the change in phraseology was the fear among some Republicans that inclusion of specific protection for office-holding would have implied that the right to hold office was not subsumed within the right to vote, and that this concession would have undermined the effort to deal with the exclusion of duly-elected African Americans from the state legislature in Georgia. Amar, "Jury Service as Political Participation," pp. 229–230.

This explanation does not withstand close scrutiny. Admittedly, some Republicans did believe that the right to vote carried with it the right to hold of-

For Sumner himself, the lack of a specific constitutional provision authorizing Congress to regulate juries was only a minor inconvenience; throughout the Reconstruction era, he consistently maintained that the Declaration of Independence was legally binding on Congress and the state governments, and that the Declaration by its terms forbade all racial discrimination. The equally radical Senator George M. Boutwell derived a similar principle from the Privileges and Immunities Clause of the Fourteenth Amendment:

> What is the first privilege of [a citizen] of the United States? That he is the equal before the law of every other citizen.... Therefore, while we cannot go into the States and say what the rights of citizens of the State in the State shall be, whenever there is a law in a State or a provision of its constitution which secures to citizens generally their rights and discriminates generally against other citizens, that discrimination is...against those citizens as citizens of the United States and [Congress has the power under the Fourteenth Amendment to] secure to our citizens...their

---

fice, and were *therefore willing* to accept an amendment that did not explicitly protect the right to hold office. See, for example, *Congressional Globe*, 40th Cong., 3d sess. (1869) at 1425–1426 (remarks of Rep. Boutwell) and 1625 (remarks of Sen. Howard). However, this sentiment was far from unanimous, and a number of radical Republican Senators complained bitterly about the omission of protection for office-holding from the report of the Conference Committee. See, for example, ibid. at 1296 (remarks of Sen. Wilson), 1628 (remarks of Sen. Morton), and 1629 (remarks of Sen. Sawyer). Moreover, the explanation of Republican Senator William M. Stewart of Nevada—the floor manager of the amendment—makes clear that the purpose of the change in language was to ensure that the proposal would be supported by some more conservative Republicans who might have opposed an office-holding provision (ibid. at 1629). The implausibility of Amar's theory is further demonstrated by the fact that no Republican articulated a Fifteenth Amendment theory in support of the jury service provision of the Civil Rights Bill. In short, his view is simply inconsistent with the historical record.

> rights under the laws of the States as citizens of the United States [including the right to sit on a jury].[26]

By contrast, other, less radical Republicans sought to craft a more limited theory that justified the jury service provision. For example, Senator George F. Edmunds of Vermont analogized the right to sit on a jury with the right to testify in court:

> If a juryman is an officer of a State and holds a political office in the constitutional sense, there would be a great deal of force in the argument against interfering with jurors in State courts.... [However] a juryman is a man; he is called in by the name of a man and not by the name of an official; and he is no more an officer than a witness is, not a bit; and if it be not constitutional to say that there shall be equal rights in the calling of witnesses, then it must follow that there must be equal rights in the same degree as in the selection of jurors.[27]

Arguments such as these shifted the focus from the rights of the person to serve on the jury to those of the person being tried. Republican Senator John Sherman of Ohio made this point even more clearly. Sherman conceded that "the right to sit on a jury is a right which no man can claim as a matter of right. It is rather a burden, rather a duty." At the same time, however, he supported the jury service provision on the ground that "it is the right of the person accused to have an impartial trial; that men of his own race, color or condition shall not be excluded on that account." Senator Oliver H.P.T. Morton of Indiana took a similar tack:

> Take the case of a [state] where colored men are not allowed to sit upon a jury. A colored man is on trial. He is to be tried by a jury of white men, perhaps for a

---

26. *Congressional Globe*, 43d Cong., 2d sess., 1793 (1875).

27. Ibid., 43d Cong., 1st sess., 1866 (1875). To the same effect, see ibid., 42d Cong., 2d sess., 820 (1872) (remarks of Sen. Morton).

> wrong inflicted upon a white person. He is to be tried by a jury that have prejudices of race against him, that are now especially, and have been for a few years past excited against him because he has attempted to be clothed with new rights. I ask if this colored man, to be tried by a jury of white men from which all colored men have been excluded, can be said in any sense to have "the equal protection of the law?"[28]

Most Republicans accepted arguments such as these, and thus voted to include the jury provision in the Civil Rights Act of 1875.

The passage did not end the debate over the constitutionality of the jury service provision. Instead, it shifted that debate to the courts. The outcome of the judicial process sent somewhat mixed signals. In its 1879 decisions in *Ex Parte Virginia*[29] and *Strauder v. West Virginia*,[30] the Supreme Court sided with Congress and rejected constitutional challenges to this portion of the Civil Rights Act of 1875. At the same time, in a companion case, the Court would interpret the statute in a manner that substantially limited the practical import of the *Virginia* and *Strauder* decisions.

Virginia was a petition for a writ of habeas corpus from a state judge who had been indicted for allegedly violating the Civil Rights Act by systematically excluding blacks from jury lists that he had prepared. The case raised two analytically distinct problems of federal-state relations. The first was the substantive question of whether the federal government could constitutionally require the states to allow blacks to serve on juries. The second was the institutional question of whether federal law could punish a state official for performance of the duties required of him by state law.

Essentially restating the position taken by Democrats and con-

---

28. Ibid., 42d Cong., 2d sess., 844, 845, 847 (1872). To the same effect, see ibid., 43d Cong., 1st sess., 3455 (1874) (remarks of Sen. Frelinghuysen).

29. 100 U.S. 339 (1879).

30. 100 U.S. 303 (1879).

servative Republicans in Congress, Democratic Justice Stephen J. Field delivered a sharply worded attack on the constitutionality of the Civil Rights Act. In part, his opinion was based upon the view that the principles of American federalism developed in *Kentucky v. Dennison* and later cases barred direct federal legislative coercion of state officials performing official functions under any circumstances. Field declared, "Nothing...could have a greater tendency to destroy the independence and autonomy of the States; reduce them to a humiliating and degrading dependence upon the central government; engender constant irritation; and destroy that domestic tranquility which it was one of the objects of the Constitution to ensure."[31]

Field's primary focus, however, was on the claim that the federal government lacked authority to prescribe the qualifications for jurors in state proceedings. After describing the principle that the federal government is one of enumerated powers, he declared:

> [I]f we look into the Constitution, we shall not find a single word, from its opening to its concluding line, nor in any of the amendments in force before the close of the civil war, nor...in those subsequently adopted, which authorizes any interference by Congress with the states in the administration of their governments, and the enforcement of their laws with respect to any matter over which jurisdiction was not surrendered to the United States.

Field asserted further, "To every State...there must be, with reference to the subjects over which it has jurisdiction, absolute free-

---

31. Ibid., pp. 358–360, 358, citing *Kentucky v. Dennison*, 65 U.S. 66 (1861) (Field, J., dissenting).

In making this argument, Field relied not only on *Dennison*, but also on *The Collector v. Day*, 78 U.S. (11 Wall.) 113 (1870). In *Day*, the Court held that the principle of state autonomy barred federal taxation of the salary of a state judicial official.

dom from all external interference in the exercise of its legislative, judicial, and executive authority."[32]

Field then turned specifically to the contention that the Fourteenth Amendment had significantly modified this principle. The essence of his argument was that "a change so radical in the relation between the Federal and State authorities, as would justify legislation interfering with the independent action of the different departments of the State governments, in all matters over which the States retain jurisdiction, was never contemplated by the [Reconstruction] amendments." Drawing on the distinction between civil and political rights, he argued that, the right to serve on juries was a political right, and that while the Fourteenth Amendment guaranteed civil rights to all persons, "[it] left to the States to determine to whom the possession of political powers should be intrusted [*sic*]." Field ended his opinion by noting that the Equal Protection Clause—after the decision in *The Slaughterhouse Cases,* the only plausible source of authority for the Civil Rights Act—applied to both aliens and citizens, and pointed out that the same line of reasoning that supported the result in *Virginia* would also seem to require states to allow aliens to serve on juries.[33]

Field, however, was able to gain only the vote of fellow Democrat Samuel Nelson. Speaking through William Strong, the seven Republicans on the Court took a quite different view of the impact of the Fourteenth Amendment on the federal structure. In sharp contrast to *Slaughterhouse,* the majority opinion in *Virginia* focused primarily on the nationalizing impact of the amendment. Strong contended that "[the Reconstruction amendments] are intended to be, what they really are, limitations of the power of the States and enlargements of the power of Congress" and that enforcement of the rights guaranteed by the amendments "is no invasion of State sovereignty." While conceding "in the general"

32. *Virginia,* 100 U.S. at 353–357, 357, 362.
33. Ibid., pp. 367, 368, 368–369.

that "the selection of jurors for her courts and the administration of her laws belong to each State," Strong found justification for the Civil Rights Act of 1875 in the flip side of American federalism—the principle that "in exercising her rights, a State cannot disregard the limitations which the Federal Constitution has applied to her power." Turning to the institutional concern with federal coercion of state officials, Strong contended that "[a] State acts by its legislative, its executive, or its judicial authorities. It can act in no other way. The constitutional provision, therefore, must mean that no agency of the State, or of the officers or agents by whom its powers are exerted shall deny to any person within its jurisdiction the equal protection of the laws." He concluded that, therefore, Congress must have authority to provide penalties for those officials who violate the principles of the Fourteenth Amendment.[34]

Strong dealt more specifically with the issue of juries in *Strauder*, which came to the Court as a companion case to *Virginia*. *Strauder* dealt with a statute derived from the Civil Rights Acts of 1866 and 1870, which provided for removal of state-court actions to federal court by defendants who would be denied or could not enforce a right secured to them by a "law providing for...equal rights." In the trial, Strauder, an African American from West Virginia, was accused of killing his wife. Under West Virginia state law, only whites were allowed to serve on juries. The defendant claimed that this exclusion was inconsistent with both the Civil Rights Act of 1866 and the Fourteenth Amendment and that he was therefore entitled to the benefit of the removal provision. The state court denied his motion, and Strauder was convicted of murder. He argued that the state court's refusal to remove the case to federal court vitiated his conviction.

Holding that the case should have been removed, Strong's reasoning tracked the arguments of those who supported the inclusion of the jury discrimination provision in the Civil Rights Act of 1875. He first contended:

34. Ibid., pp. 345, 346, 347, 348.

> The very fact that [African Americans] are singled out and expressly denied by a statute all right to participate in the administration of the law, as jurors... is practically a brand upon them, affixed by the law, an assertion of their inferiority, and a stimulant to that race prejudice which is an impediment to securing to individuals of the race that equal justice which the law aims to secure to all others.

In addition, Strong adopted the views of Sherman and Morton, asserting that the statute denied equal protection to black defendants themselves and arguing, "It is not easy to comprehend how it can be said that while every white man is entitled to a trial by a jury selected from persons of his own race or color, or, rather, selected without discrimination against his color, and a negro is not, the latter is equally protected by the law with the former."[35]

The significance of *Strauder* and *Virginia* for constitutional theory cannot be overstated. The Court went well beyond the argument that it was simply protecting the rights of African American defendants; instead, in contending that the exclusion of African Americans was unconstitutional because it was "an assertion of their inferiority," Strong also seemed to indicate that all state laws that discriminated against blacks were unconstitutional. Thus, *Strauder* and *Virginia* cannot simply be dismissed as cases in which, in the words of Benno C. Schmidt, the Court "freed the fourteenth amendment from the narrowest readings of its legislative history and looked for meaning in the broad purposes that the language connoted [and thereby] measure[d] the sweep of equal protection in a functional and broadly historical perspective."[36] Rather, the *Strauder* Court implicitly rejected one of the most fundamental premises underlying section 1 of the Fourteenth Amendment—that the section did not cover politi-

---

35. *Strauder*, 100 U.S. at 308, 309.
36. Schmidt, "Juries, Jurisdiction and Race Discrimination," pp. 1428–1429.

cal rights.[37] Moreover, in sanctioning the use of criminal penalties against state officials, the Court vindicated the power of Congress to intrude deeply into the structure of state governments to enforce the strictures imposed by section 1. In short, the jury discrimination cases stand as a clear reaffirmation of the view—first suggested in *Slaughterhouse*—that where racial discrimination is at issue, ordinary concerns of federalism should at times be overborne in constitutional analysis.

Nonetheless, many commentators have downplayed the significance of *Virginia* and *Strauder*, choosing instead to emphasize the decision in the companion case of *Virginia v. Rives.* Like *Strauder*, *Rives* challenged the refusal of a state court to grant a petition for removal that was based upon a claim that blacks were improperly excluded from a jury in a criminal case. In *Rives*, however, the relevant state statutes did not prohibit blacks from serving on juries; instead, the gravamen of the defendant's claim was that the presiding judge made an independent decision to limit jury service to whites, in direct contravention of state law.[38]

The disposition of *Rives* was strongly influenced by the reformulation of the removal statute during the compilation project that culminated in the passage of the *Revised Statutes of 1875*. In theory, the purpose of the compilation was only to systematize and clarify existing law; the compilers were not to make substantive changes. However, the compilers inexplicably made a major change in the removal provision. As initially formulated in 1866, the provision incorporated by reference the procedures of the Habeas Corpus Suspension Act of 1863, which in turn allowed both pretrial and postjudgment removal—a point clearly re-

---

37. Lino A. Graglia, "'Interpreting' the Constitution: Posner on Bork," *Stanford Law Review* 44 [1992]: 1019–1050 at 1042, suggests that this distinction was undermined by the adoption of the Fifteenth Amendment. This contention is vastly overstated; as we have seen, the drafters of the Fifteenth Amendment explicitly rejected broad protection of political rights in favor of the current, narrowly drawn provision.

38. 100 U.S. 313 (1880).

flected in Trumbull's only systematic exposition of the removal process.[39] However, the *Revised Statutes* provided only for pretrial removal. Against this background, the Court unanimously held that removal was not available in *Rives*. Once again speaking for the united Republican majority, Strong noted that the removal statute required a defendant to demonstrate *before trial* that he was unable to enforce his "equal civil rights" in the judicial tribunals of the state. He argued that where (as in *Rives*) state statutes forbade discrimination against blacks, one should presume that the defendant could vindicate his rights in either the state trial courts or the state appellate courts.[40] Thus, he concluded, in those cases removal to federal court should not be available.

The *Rives* Court clearly rejected a plausible expansive reading of the removal jurisdiction. Further, the decision greatly limited the effectiveness of removal as a weapon against discrimination in jury selection. Some commentators have taken these observations a step further, suggesting that *Rives* was simply a further reflection of the justices' willingness to sacrifice the interests of blacks in order to reinforce both the political settlement of 1877 and the traditional structure of federalism.[41]

As Schmidt has persuasively argued, such contentions are overstated.[42] The scholars who embrace this view take *Rives* out of context. If the members of the Republican majority had in fact been intent on protecting the traditional structure of federalism, they could simply have held that Congress lacked all power to regulate the relevant activity—just as they were to hold only three years later in *The Civil Rights Cases*. Moreover, as Strong's opinion suggests,[43] the threat of criminal sanctions rather than removal

39. *Congressional Globe*, 39th Cong., 1st sess., 1759 (1866).

40. *Rives*, 100 U.S. at 318–319, 320–321.

41. See, for example, Hyman and Wiecek, *Equal Justice under Law*, pp. 494–495.

42. Schmidt, "Juries, Jurisdiction and Race Discrimination," pp. 1402, 1433–1440.

43. *Rives*, 100 U.S. at 321.

was viewed as the main source of protection for the right of blacks to be free from state-imposed racial discrimination.[44] Of course, one might still conclude that the Court erred in deciding *Rives* as it did.[45] Nonetheless, to infer that the Republican justices had no real commitment to eliminating jury discrimination misconstrues the import of the decision. Instead, the decision is best understood as a case in which the justices' attachment to distinctively legal principles overcame their commitment to racial justice.

The impact of distinctively legal principles emerged even more clearly in *Williams v. Mississippi.*[46] In *Williams*, an African American who had been convicted of murder sought to have his conviction overturned on the ground that the grand jury that had indicted him was chosen in a manner calculated to exclude blacks from service. This argument was premised on two points. First, it was an undisputed fact that the Mississippi state constitution required all jurors to be eligible to vote. Second, the facially neutral constitutional requirement that prospective voters be able to both read and understand any provision of the state constitution that the registrar might choose to read to them had actually been adopted with the purpose of providing registrars with the authority to prevent blacks from registering. The Supreme Court unanimously rejected the constitutional challenge. Speaking for the Court, Justice Joseph McKenna dismissed the allegation that the registration scheme had been adopted for a discriminatory purpose as irrelevant, declaring that "with this we have no concern, unless the purpose is executed by the constitution or laws or by those who administer them."

Both Michael Les Benedict and Benno C. Schmidt have argued that *Williams* is a case of extraordinary doctrinal significance, with Benedict suggesting that the case reflects a substantial departure from principles established by the Waite Court and

---

44. *Congressional Globe*, 39th Cong., 1st sess., 475 (1866).
45. Schmidt, "Juries, Jurisdiction and Discrimination," pp. 1433–1440, is sharply critical of *Rives* without impugning the motives of the Court.
46. 170 U.S. 213 (1898).

Schmidt arguing that the Court's rejection of intent-based analysis was a major doctrinal innovation.[47] However, the *Williams* analysis had been foreshadowed by the congressional discussions of the Fifteenth Amendment. For example, Republican Representative Samuel A. Shellabarger of Ohio complained that a simple prohibition on racial discrimination would leave states free to exclude substantially all African Americans from voting by imposing facially neutral qualifications based on education or property, and Republican Senator Jacob M. Howard of Michigan conceded that states could adopt any criteria that were imposed on all potential voters equally.[48] Further, the approach of the *Williams* Court was nothing more than a reiteration of the principles that the Waite Court had developed in a series of cases dealing with discrimination against natives of China.[49]

As has already been noted, prejudice against the Chinese was rampant in the late nineteenth century. This prejudice sharply limited their employment opportunities. In a few less-desirable industries, however, they came to dominate the market in California, where the Chinese population was concentrated. The commercial laundry industry was one such area of Chinese dominance; for example, in 1880 it was estimated that of 320 laundries in San Francisco, approximately 240 were owned by Chinese, and in 1882, one anti-Chinese group of trade unionists estimated that commercial laundries in San Francisco employed 5,107 Chinese and only 615 whites.[50] This industry thus presented a tempting target for the anti-Chinese political movement.

---

47. Benedict, "Preserving Federalism," p. 73; Schmidt, "Juries, Jurisdiction and Discrimination," pp. 1468–1470.

48. *Congressional Globe*, 40th Cong., 1st sess., app. 97–99, 1009, 1010 (1867).

49. The discussion which follows is taken from Earl M. Maltz, "The Federal Government and the Problem of Chinese Rights in the Era of the Fourteenth Amendment," *Harvard Journal of Law and Public Policy* 17 (1994):223–249.

50. *Yick Wo v. Hopkins*, 118 U.S. 356, 358–359 (1886); Alexander P. Saxton, *The Indispensable Enemy: Labor and the Anti-Chinese Movement in California* (Berkeley, 1972), p. 180.

Two San Francisco city ordinances dealing specifically with laundries generated litigation in the Supreme Court. The first, adopted in 1880, required the approval of the city Board of Supervisors in order to operate a laundry in a building not constructed of brick or stone. The second, adopted in 1884, placed a number of restrictions on the operations of such laundries, including a prohibition on the washing and ironing of clothes between the hours of ten in the evening and six in the morning. Constitutional challenges to both of these ordinances ultimately came before the Supreme Court; because of the vagaries of litigation, the Court first adjudicated the constitutionality of the 1884 ordinance.

The first case in which the Court passed on the merits of the ordinance did not directly implicate the issue of racial discrimination. Rather, in *Barbier v. Connolly*, a non-Chinese laundry worker argued that the ordinance violated the Fourteenth Amendment because it discriminated between workers in different businesses and between workers who performed their functions at different times of the day. Rejecting the challenge for a unanimous Court, Justice Stephen J. Field characterized the ordinance as "a police regulation within the competency of any municipality possessed of the ordinary powers belonging to such bodies" and declared that the Fourteenth Amendment "was [not] designed to interfere with the power of the State, sometimes termed its police power, to prescribe regulations to promote the health, peace, morals, education and good order of the State." At the same time, however, invoking an important principle of antebellum jurisprudence, Field asserted that the amendment would invalidate "[c]lass legislation, discriminating against some and favoring others."[51]

Soon Hing v. Cowley, decided the same term as *Barbier*, began

---

51. 113 U.S. 27, 28, 33, 31 (1885).

The first case to actually reach the Court was *Ex Parte Tom Tong*, 108 U.S. 552 (1883), which was a challenge to the 1880 ordinance. However, *Tom Tong* was dismissed on procedural grounds.

to explore the limits of the concept of class legislation. In *Soon Hing*, a Chinese laundry worker challenged the same prohibition that had been upheld in *Barbier*. However, in addition to raising arguments analogous to those that the Court had already rejected, the Chinese worker claimed that the ordinance was unconstitutional because it was adopted not for any legitimate purpose, but rather to drive the Chinese from the laundry industry in which they held such a prominent position. Once more speaking for a unanimous Court, Field also rejected this argument, asserting that

> the rule is general with reference to the enactments of all legislative bodies that the courts cannot inquire into the motives of all legislators in passing them, except as may be disclosed on the face of the acts, or inferable from their operation, considered with reference to the condition of the country and existing legislation.... [E]ven if the motives of the supervisors were as alleged, the ordinance would not be thereby changed from a legitimate police regulation, unless in its enforcement it is made to operate only against the class mentioned.[52]

In other words, in Field's view, with only the rarest exceptions, facial discrimination would be the sole determinate of equal protection violations. Thus, he found the San Francisco ordinance to be constitutionally unexceptionable.

By contrast, in the following year, the requirement that wooden laundries receive the approval of the Board of Supervisors was invalidated in *Yick Wo v. Hopkins*. While race played little direct role in most of Justice Stanley Matthews's opinion for the Court, Matthews did refer to the issue at the end of the opinion. He noted that because the record reflected the actual operation of the challenged ordinances, "we are not obliged to reason from the probable to the actual, and pass upon the validity of the

52. *Soon Hing v. Cowley*, 113 U.S. 703, 710, 710–711 (1885).

ordinances complained of, as tried merely by the opportunities which their terms afford, of unequal and unjust discrimination in their administration." He concluded that

> whatever may have been the intent of the ordinances as adopted, they are applied by the public ordinances charged with their administration... with a mind so unequal and oppressive as to amount to a practical denial by the State of the equal protection of the laws.... Though the law itself be fair on its face and impartial in its appearance, yet, it is administered by public authority with an evil eye and an unequal hand, so as practically to make unjust and illegal discriminations between persons in similar circumstances, material to their rights, the denial of equal justice is still within the prohibition of the Constitution.... No reason whatever, except the will of the supervisors is assigned why [the Chinese] should not be permitted to carry on, in the accustomed manner, their harmless and useful occupation, on which they depend for a livelihood.... No reason for [the discriminatory pattern] is shown, and the conclusion cannot be resisted, that no reason for it exists except hostility to the race and nationality to which the petitioners belong, and which in the eye of the law is not justified. The discrimination is, therefore, illegal.[53]

This condemnation of discriminatory application must be read against the background of the Court's reasoning in *Soon Hing*, decided the same term and cited with approval in *Yick Wo* itself. There the Court had indicated that statistical evidence could invalidate an otherwise unexceptionable regulation only when "its enforcement it is made to operate *only* against the [relevant] class."[54] The *Yick Wo* fact pattern fit this exception almost

53. *Yick Wo v. Hopkins*, 118 U.S. 356, 373–374 (1886).
54. *Soon Hing*, 113 U.S. at 710–711.

perfectly; given the unexplained gross disparity in result, the only plausible conclusion was that the city officials were singling out Chinese launderers for unfavorable treatment.

When *Williams v. Mississippi* came before the Court in 1898, the constitutional challenge was governed by the principles established in the Chinese laundry cases. The refusal of the Court to consider the motive of the legislature was mandated by *Soon Hing*. Conversely, *Yick Wo* was distinguished on the ground that the *Williams* plaintiff had produced no evidence of race-based enforcement of the registration requirements. Thus, in declaring that the constitutional challenge in *Williams* was without merit because "the constitution of Mississippi and its statutes... do not on their face discriminate against the races, and it has not been shown that their actual administrative was evil, only that evil was possible under them,"[55] Justice McKenna did not break any new doctrinal ground. Instead, the *Williams* Court simply relied upon well-established principles of legal analysis.

At the same time, however, it cannot be denied that the political and jurisprudential atmosphere in which *Williams* was decided was far different than that which had produced the decisions in *Virginia* and *Strauder*. On racial issues, the Fuller Court was indeed substantially more conservative than its predecessor. These differences emerged in a number of different contexts. For example, in 1903, the Court ignored the contrary language in *Yarbrough* and concluded that Congress could not constitutionally reach private, racially discriminatory acts that were designed to prevent African Americans from voting.[56] The point is illustrated even more clearly by the evolution of the Court's treatment of segregation in the instrumentalities of public transportation.

---

55. Ibid., pp. 223, 225.
56. *James v. Bowman*, 190 U.S. 127 (1903).

Chapter 6

The Road to *Plessy*: The Reconstruction Amendments and the Right to Use Public Transportation

All legal scholars would agree that *The Slaughterhouse Cases*, *Cruikshank*, *Strauder*, and the like were of considerable significance in the development of the law of the Fourteenth Amendment. However, in terms of fame (or infamy), these decisions are dwarfed by another landmark of late-nineteenth-century jurisprudence. That case, of course, is the much-maligned 1896 decision in *Plessy v. Ferguson*, where the Court rejected a constitutional challenge to a statute that mandated segregation in public transportation.[1]

Like the other cases interpreting the Reconstruction amendments, *Plessy* was decided against the background of a substantial body of jurisprudence that evolved before the drafting of the Fourteenth Amendment.[2] That jurisprudence, much of which de-

1. Charles A. Lofgren, *The Plessy Case: A Legal-Historical Interpretation* (New York, 1990), is the definitive study of *Plessy*.

2. Much of the first part of this chapter is taken from Earl M. Maltz, "'Separate but Equal' and the Law of Common Carriers in the Era of the Fourteenth Amendment," *Rutgers Law Journal* 17 (1986): 553–568.

veloped in connection with the power of eminent domain, established the principle that common carriers had a different legal status than ordinary private enterprises. The basis of this unusual status was the view that, although common carriers may be private in form, they perform a public function and thus for many purposes should be considered an arm of the state. This theory was universally accepted during the nineteenth century. Thus, for example, Justice Samuel Nelson noted in *New Jersey Steam Navigation Co. v. Merchants' Bank* that a common carrier "is in the exercise of a sort of public office, and has public duties to perform."[3] The Supreme Judicial Court of Massachusetts was more expansive in *Inhabitants of Worcester v. Western Railroad Corp.*, arguing:

> The establishment of [a railroad] is regarded as a public work, established by public authority, intended for the public use and benefit, the use of which is secured to the whole community, and constitutes, therefore, . . . a public easement. . . . It is true that the real and personal property, necessary to the establishment and management of the railroad, is vested in the corporation; but it is in trust, for the public.[4]

While not completely vitiating the idea that common carriers were private property, this difference in status led to the imposition of special obligations on the operators of such instrumentalities. Although private parties generally were free to refuse to contract with whomever they pleased, a common carrier was "bound to take [one wishing passage] as a passenger on board, if [the common carrier] had suitable accommodations, and there was no reasonable objection to the character or conduct of the [passenger]." At the same time, however, the right to passage was "not an unlimited right" but was "subject to such reasonable regulations as

---

3. 47 U.S. (6 How.) 344, 382–383 (1848).

4. 45 Mass. (4 Met.) 564, 566 (1842). In addition, see cases cited in *Civil Rights Cases*, 109 U.S. 3, 37–39 (1883) (Harlan, J., dissenting); Robert Hutchinson, *A Treatise on the Law of Carriers* (Chicago, 1882), p. 30 n. 2.

the proprietors may prescribe, for the due accommodation of passengers and for the due arrangements of their business." Moreover, proprietors were "not bound to admit passengers on board, who refuse to obey the reasonable regulations of the [carrier] or who are guilty of gross and vulgar habits of conduct; or who make disturbances on board; or whose characters are doubtful or dissolute or suspicious [or] unequivocally bad."[5] Even prior to the Civil War, these principles generated legal challenges to the practices of common carriers that discriminated on the basis of race.[6]

Some courts distinguished between the right to be transported and the right to equal accommodations. The former alone was at issue in *State v. Kimber*. There the conductor of a street railroad was accused of assault and battery after forcibly evicting a mulatto who sought to travel in the railroad car. His defense was that the mulatto was rightfully excluded from the car as "a person of color" and that the company that operated the railroad was under no obligation to make transportation facilities available to her. An Ohio trial court rejected this contention, quoting Republican legal scholar Edward L. Pierce for the proposition that a common carrier "cannot make unreasonable discriminations between persons soliciting its means of conveyance, as by refusing them on account of... complexion, race [or] nativity."[7]

When considering the issue of equal accommodations, however, the Michigan Supreme Court took a different view in *Day v. Owen*. There, although agreeing to accept an African American passenger, a steamer owner denied him the right to accommodation in a cabin. Instead, the passenger was required to ride on deck. Finding this requirement to be lawful, the court argued:

> The right to be carried is one thing—the privileges of

---

5. *Jencks v. Coleman*, 13 F. Cas. 442, 443 (C.C.D.R.I. 1835) (no. 7258) (Story, J.).

6. These challenges are described in Litwack, *North of Slavery*, pp. 106–112.

7. 4 Ohio Dec. 197, 197–198 (Hamilton County Common Pleas 1859), quoting Edward L. Pierce, *A Treatise on American Railroad Law* (New York, 1857).

> a passenger on board of the boat, what part of it may be occupied by him, or he have the right to use, is another thing. The two rights are very different. The latter, and not the former right, is subject to reasonable rules and regulations, and is, where such rules and regulations exist, to be determined by them.

In *Day*, the court found that the defendant had produced ample evidence that the rule was "calculated to render the transportation most comfortable and least annoying to... a large majority of the passengers ordinarily carried." To deny the owner the authority to make such a rule "would be an interference with a carrier's control over his own property in his own way, not necessary to the performance of his duty to the public as a carrier."[8]

No other state court of last resort dealt with similar issues prior to the Civil War. However, the *Day* approach, which reflected widely shared attitudes toward racial issues, was prominently featured in lower court decisions from other states in the antebellum era. Even during the Civil War, the free states remained hotbeds of racism. Nonetheless, in some areas the courts began to show less tolerance for segregation by common carriers. However, progress was at best uneven.

In New York City, the situation of African Americans using street railroad cars improved markedly during the war. Though African Americans were not completely excluded from these cars in the antebellum era, they were in a substantially worse position than were whites who rode the cars. African Americans were entitled to ride inside only in those cars that were clearly marked as provided for their use. In all other cars, African Americans were only allowed to ride outside, on the platform.[9]

This discrimination was challenged in a series of lawsuits in the 1850s. Initially the outlook seemed quite hopeful. In 1855,

---

8. 5 Mich. 520, 526, 527 (1858).
9. See *New York Daily Times*, May 29, 1855, p. 1, col. 6.

an African American woman who was forcibly ejected from a streetcar after vigorously objecting to the company policy of segregation obtained a judgment for damages. The judge instructed the jury that African Americans, "if sober, well-behaved, and free from disease," possessed the same rights as whites to use public transportation. Subsequent legal actions, however, produced less progressive results. In *Pennington v. Sixth Avenue Railway*—a similar case decided in 1856—the plaintiff was unsuccessful after the presiding judge adopted the *Day* approach, charging the jury that the crucial question was whether the regulation relegating blacks to the platform was reasonable. In 1858, the same result was reached in *Jenkins v. Lewis.*[10]

By 1864, however, attitudes had shifted sufficiently to allow a definitive resolution favoring African Americans who sought to desegregate the cars. The vehicle for this resolution was a disciplinary proceeding against a police officer who had honored the request of a conductor and aided in forcibly removing an African-American woman from a streetcar. The police officer was found guilty of assaulting the woman and breaking police regulations. In arriving at its decision, the disciplinary board commented that "there was no law against these people riding in the cars, and they had no right to make such a law." In response to the decision, the superintendent of the street railroad company directed that "hereafter colored people are allowed to ride in all the cars, both small and large, of this company."[11]

The situation in Philadelphia was somewhat more equivocal. In that city, street railroad companies limited African Americans

---

10. Litwack, *North of Slavery*, pp. 111–112; Mary White Ovington, *The Status of the Negro in New York* (New York, 1969); Leo H. Hirsch, "The Negro and New York, 1783–1865," *Journal of Negro History* 16 (1931): 382–473, pp. 425–426; *New York Daily Times*, Dec. 18, 1856, p. 2, col. 5; Apr. 15, 1858, p. 2, col. 4.

11. *New York Daily Times*, June 30, 1864, p. 5, col. 1. For a contrasting position, see the views of the New York-based *Journal of Commerce*, quoted in *National Anti-Slavery Standard*, July 2, 1864, p. 1, col. 2.

to riding on the platforms of the cars.[12] In 1861, a local court found the restriction unobjectionable in *Goines v. M'Candless*. The *Goines* court emphasized that despite their public aspects, street railroads were privately owned enterprises. It stated:

> What we have to decide in this case... is not whether the law does or should exclude negroes from passenger cars, nor yet whether they can be excluded from them consistently with the natural equity which should prevail between man and man... but whether, when a passenger railroad company thinks it proper to exclude them, the law ought to intervene and compel their admittance.

Moreover, the court suggested that the regulation was a wise one:

> When it becomes necessary to lay down rules for the government and association of men in public, public sentiment must be consulted...as a necessary element, without which the problem cannot be solved correctly, or any permanent good attained in practice. And when a nation suffers as ours does, from the misfortune of having two races within its bosom, one dominant, the other enslaved or subject; one long civilized, and the other emerging from the shades of barbarism, and each indelibly marked by diversities of manners, color and physiognomy, there is much in the relation between them which must be left to the lessons of experience, and the tribunal of public opinion, which cannot be arbitrarily forced or hastened, without producing or augmenting repulsion and antipathy, and endangering a collision, which must necessarily prove disastrous to the weaker party.[13]

Four years later, in *Derry v. Lowry*, another Philadelphia judge

---

12. *National Anti-Slavery Standard*, Aug. 20, 1864, p. 1, cols. 5–6; Dec. 17, 1864, p. 1, col. 6; p. 2, col. 1.

13. 4 Phila. Rep. 255, 256, 257 (1861).

took a quite different view. *Derry* was an assault action arising from the forcible eviction of an African-American woman from a streetcar. The defense was based on a company regulation prohibiting African Americans from riding inside the cars. While the relevance of the possibility that the woman could ride on the platform was not mentioned, the language of the court was sufficiently broad to condemn all racial discrimination by common carriers:

> The true principle is that a corporation created for the carriage of passengers has no right to exclude any class of persons, as a class, from the benefits of its mode of transportation; it may *for cause* either by or without a regulation exclude individuals. A corporation of this description might as well undertake to make nationality or religion a ground of exclusion, as color;... such an exclusion would not be tolerated by any intelligent tribunal; yet... a question can be seriously made before a court and jury and practically enforced at the bar of public opinion, as to the right of an individual conductor, or a company, to turn persons out of the passenger cars of the city with force and violence because of their complexion. Than this, nothing can be more unreasonable; nothing... is a clearer or grosser violation of the plainest principles of the law and of the rights of individuals.

By the end of the Civil War, the *Derry* approach was generally followed in the Philadelphia courts.[14]

Despite its doctrinal significance, *Derry* did not directly address the issue of whether the railroad companies were required to

---

14. 6 Phila. Rep. 30, 32 (Common Pleas, 1865) (emphasis in original); *National Anti-Slavery Standard*, Mar. 31, 1866, p. 2, col. 1.

A similar result was reached in a California case. *Congressional Globe*, 38th Cong., 2d sess., 916 (1865) (remarks of Sen. Sumner); *National Anti-Slavery Standard*, Dec. 24, 1864, p. 1, col. 4.

allow African Americans to ride in the same cars as whites rather than simply to provide separate but equal facilities. Two years later, this question came before the Pennsylvania Supreme Court in *Westchester and Philadelphia Railroad Co. v. Miles.* In *Miles*, a Philadelphia carrier had allowed an African-American woman to ride on its railroad; the conductor, however, had required her to take a seat at one end of a car rather than in the middle, as she wished. The seat to which she was directed "was in all respects... comfortable, safe and convenient... not inferior in any of these respects to the one she was directed to leave in." While conceding that "no one can be excluded from carriage by a public carrier on account of color," the court found that in the absence of contrary statutory authority, the railroad was entitled to regulate seating in this manner. The opinion focused on the right of the carrier to make reasonable regulations and continued:

> The natural separation of the races is... an undeniable fact, and all social organizations which lead to their amalgamation are repugnant to the law of nature.... Following the order of Divine Providence, human authority ought not to compel these widely separated races to intermix. The right of such to be free from social contact is as clear as to be free from intermarriage. The former may be less repulsive as a condition, but not less entitled to protection as a right.[15]

The pattern of decisions from *Day* to *Miles* demonstrates that in the 1860s, the rights of African Americans with respect to public transportation were somewhat uncertain. All agreed that blacks could not be totally excluded from common carriers; the authorities disagreed, however, not only on the segregation issue but also on the question of whether the facilities provided to blacks were required to be equal to those provided to whites. Given the prevalent Negrophobia of the era, it should not be surprising that a

15. 55 Pa. 209, 211, 213–214 (1867).

number of courts countenanced discrimination against free blacks. Nonetheless, beginning in the 1860s, Congress began to act directly against segregation in public transportation.

The campaign against segregation in the District of Columbia street railroad was spearheaded by Senator Charles Sumner of Massachusetts. Beginning in 1863, Sumner pressed for a requirement that charters of local transportation companies include language providing that "no person shall be excluded from the cars [or at times 'any car'] on account of color." In making his arguments, Sumner was able to focus on incidents such as the case of Major A. T. Augusta, an African American surgeon serving in the Union Army. Augusta attempted to board a car on a street railroad. He was informed that he could not ride inside the car, but instead would have to ride with the driver in the front of the car. After refusing to accept this decision, Augusta was ejected from the car.[16]

Despite incidents such as this, Sumner's proposals faced opposition. One group of senators—primarily Democrats—defended the right of the railroads to place African Americans in separate cars. The most extreme position was taken by Democratic Senator Willard Saulsbury of Delaware. Referring to the Augusta affair, Saulsbury stated:

> I most heartily approve of the action of the officer on board that railroad car. I think he deserves the thanks of the community. When these negroes go about sticking their heads into railroad cars, and among white people... I think an officer is perfectly right in telling them they have no business there.[17]

---

16. *Congressional Globe,* 37th Cong., 2d sess., 1324 (1863); ibid., 38th Cong., 1st sess., 553 (1864); *National Anti-Slavery Standard,* Feb. 20, 1864, p. 2, col. 5.

17. *Congressional Globe,* 38th Cong., 1st sess., 817 (1863). To the same effect, see ibid., p. 3134 (remarks of Sen. Powell).

Taking a more moderate view, conservative Republican James R. Doolittle of Wisconsin tracked the reasoning of *Day v. Owen*:

> [I]n a community where nearly half the population are colored people and the other half of the population are white people, if it is for the convenience of the traveling public that cars should be separated, and seats for colored persons provided in one car and seats for white persons in another, there is nothing in it that tramples on anybody's rights; nothing which does not serve the convenience of the public.[18]

Unlike Doolittle, most Republican senators seemed to accept the principle that streetcars should not be segregated by race. Nonetheless, some opposed Sumner because they believed that his proposals would be unnecessary or ineffectual. Thus, for example, apparently agreeing with Democratic Senator Reverdy Johnson's assertion that "[a]s I understand the charter [of the railroad company], it contains no provision at all by which there is in the company any power to distinguish between... two classes of people [on the basis of race]," Senator Lyman Trumbull of Illinois declared, "I am willing to go for any measure that can accomplish good; but the right of the negro to ride in the cars upon [the] city railroad[s] is not affected in the least by the [Sumner proposals]." By contrast, Republican Senator Waitman T. Willey of West Virginia argued: "[T]his is a matter that we cannot regulate by law, practically. It is a matter to be regulated by the interests of the company, the convenience of the people, and especially the tastes of the people." Still other Republicans contended that the issue was too trivial to warrant the Senate's attention; Senator James W. Grimes of Iowa suggested that African Americans were "more outraged [by] the interference of white men with the cars devoted to the exclusive use of colored people" than by exclusion from all-white cars, and Senator John Sherman of Ohio declared

---

18. Ibid., p. 1159. To the same effect, see ibid., pp. 1158–1159 (remarks of Sen. Carlile).

that "this thing of tinkering constantly with these little charters, simply because somebody is dissatisfied and has not had his way about it, is one of the most disgusting kinds of legislation."[19]

These objections were made against the background of the political dangers inherent in forcing the railroads to allow whites and African Americans to ride in the same cars. Democrats portrayed the Sumner proposals as typical of a Republican commitment to a principle of "Negro equality" that included social as well as legal equality. Most Republicans vigorously denied this assertion, instead contending that they wished only to guarantee African Americans their basic civil rights. Nonetheless, the debate over segregation on the street railroads provided Democrats with an opportunity to portray the Republican party as concerned with protecting African Americans at the expense of prerogatives of whites.[20]

Ultimately, these political considerations were not decisive for most Republicans; by early 1865, Sumner had succeeded in overcoming the opposition and attaching his provisos to the charters of all street railroads in the District of Columbia. Moreover, in 1873, the Supreme Court removed all doubt about the import of these provisos in *Washington, Alexandria & Georgetown Railroad Co. v. Brown.*[21] *Brown* dealt with a situation that was something of a cause célèbre. In 1868, Catherine Brown, an African American employee of the United States Senate, purchased a ticket to ride on a street railroad. The train that she boarded was composed of two cars. She wished to sit in the rear car, which was reserved for whites; however, a conductor ordered her to go to the forward car. When she refused to comply, a violent altercation ensued in which Ms. Brown was severely injured. The incident

19. Ibid., pp. 1156, 3132, 3131, 817, 3133–3134. Ibid., 38th Cong., 2d sess., 3831 (1864).

20. See, for example, the colloquy between Democratic Senator Thomas A. Hendricks of Indiana and Republican Senator James Harlan of Iowa, *Congressional Globe,* 38th Cong., 1st sess., 838–839 (1864).

21. 84 U.S. (17 Wall.) 445 (1873).

generated a storm of protest on the Senate floor, with one senator even calling for the revocation of the charter of the railroad. The matter was referred to the Committee on the District of Columbia for inquiry and action. Noting that the revocation would generate great public hardship, the committee recommended that Ms. Brown be left to her judicial remedies to obtain recompense for her injuries. At trial, she obtained a judgment for $1,500.[22]

An appeal from this judgment ultimately found its way to the Supreme Court. The company defended itself on the ground that its regulation was reasonable. In making this argument the company had two advantages. First, the case involved accommodations that were truly separate but equal. Each train contained two equally comfortable cars, one set aside for whites and the other for blacks. On the return trip the cars were reversed, with the car previously used for whites now reserved for blacks and vice versa. Second, the specific charter provision at issue was an early version of the Sumner proviso, prohibiting the exclusion of African Americans from "the cars" rather than "any car." As the Court noted in *Brown*, such language could plausibly be read to allow the use of separate cars. Nonetheless, the Supreme Court affirmed the lower court judgment, finding that the charter required that the company admit blacks to all cars. Thus, the principle that streetcars in the District of Columbia could not be segregated by race became firmly ensconced in the law.[23]

This result is particularly striking when viewed against the background of contemporary legislation dealing with the District of Columbia schools. During the early 1860s, Congress for the first time provided public schools for black children living in the District of Columbia. These schools, however, were not integrated; instead, a separate set of schools for black children was es-

---

22. *Congressional Globe,* 40th Cong., 2d sess., 1121–1125, 1125 (1868) (remarks of Sen. Nye); S. Rep. no. 131, 40th Cong., 2d sess., 2–3 (1868); *Brown,* 84 U.S. at 449.

23. *Brown,* 84 U.S. at 449, 447, 452.

tablished, funded by a tax on the property owned by blacks.[24] Thus, when considering congressional action with respect to street railroads, one is faced with a seeming anomaly; how can one reconcile the decision to forbid the private choice to segregate the railroad cars with the decision to mandate segregation in the governmentally operated school system? The analysis of the *Derry* court provides the framework by which this seeming inconsistency can be resolved:

> [Street railroads] are chartered for the accommodation of the community generally, and to this end the uses of the public highway of the city along and over which every person, without distinction of age or sex, or nationality or color has a right to a free and unobstructed passage is to the extent defined in the several acts of incorporation given to these companies for the construction of their roads. But these grants by the Legislature were not intended to divert the highways of the city from the purpose for which they were established; to some extent they changed the *mode* of transit over said highway; but the object of the grant was in aid of this common right of passage upon and over the streets of the city; it was to render travel more easy and convenient to those to whom the right belonged, and this right is a common right; it belongs equally to the rich and to the poor, to the black man as much as to the white man.[25]

This reasoning rests on two related principles. First, it reflects the widely shared view that common carriers are quasi-public entities. Second, unlike benefits such as public education, whose availability was generally viewed as a matter of governmental grace, the *Derry* opinion linked the right to use common carriers to the right to travel—described by a variety of authorities as one

---

24. *Congressional Globe*, 37th Cong., 2d sess., 1854, 2020, 3117 (1862).
25. 6 Phila. Rep. at 31 (emphasis in original).

of the most fundamental of all rights.[26] Thus, the argument was not that segregation was per se wrong; rather, the basic contention was that to bar any person from access to any common carrier without reasonable cause deprived that person of a portion of his fundamental right to travel. Since Republicans generally did not view racial prejudice as reasonable cause, they concluded that, absent additional justification, to deny an African American access to any street railroad car would violate his fundamental rights. Similar considerations would ultimately lead to federal legislation requiring all common carriers to desegregate their cars. However, because of the political sensitivity of the issue, legislative success came only after a protracted struggle.

The Civil Rights Act of 1866—the first statute designed to establish a nationwide ban on many forms of racial discrimination—did not specifically address the issue of racial discrimination by common carriers. The statute did, however, guarantee more generally that "citizens of every race and color... shall have the same right to make and enforce contracts... as white citizens." The application of this provision to segregation by common carriers was a matter of considerable debate.

Democrats contended that the Act would prohibit segregation by common carriers, and made this claim a centerpiece for their arguments against passage. The overblown rhetoric of Democratic Senator Garrett Davis of Kentucky exemplifies the allegations of the opposition on this point:

> On ships and steamboats the most comfortable and handsomely furnished cabins and state-rooms, the first tables, and other privileges; in public hotels the most luxuriously appointed parlors, chambers, and saloons, the most sumptuous tables, and baths; in churches not only the most softly cushioned pews,

---

26. See, for example, *Congressional Globe,* 42d Cong., 2d sess., 3191, 3192 (1872); *Corfield v. Coryell,* 6 F. Cas. 546, 551–552 (C.C.E.D. Pa. 1823); Tucker, *Blackstone's Commentaries,* 2:134.

> but the most eligible sections; on railroads, national, local, and street, not only seats, but whole cars are assigned to white persons to the exclusion of negroes and mulattoes. All these discriminations . . . [t]his bill proposes to break down.[27]

Republicans supporters of the Civil Rights Act seem to have been split on the issue. The *Germantown Telegraph*, for example, believed that the Act guaranteed blacks the right to go on public conveyances. Other Republican newspapers took a different view, however. The discussions of the issue in the *Cincinnati Commercial*—a newspaper on the conservative edge of the Republican mainstream—provide the most dramatic illustration. Initially the *Commercial* expressed grave doubts about the proposal, fearing that it might be interpreted to require the opening of "hotels, churches and theaters without distinction on the basis of color." Within a month, however, the editors of the *Commercial* abandoned their objections, having been assured by supporters of the bill, including "influential members" of the Ohio delegation, that the prohibitions would not apply to Ohio at all, and that the bill's provisions would affect only those states that had Black Codes. In other words, having noted the existence of private discriminatory customs and having decried federal efforts to abolish those customs, the *Commercial* supported the Civil Rights Act after being assured that it would have no effect on private discrimination. The *Philadelphia North American* expressed a similar understanding, asserting that the rights protected by the Act did not include the right to "go to any car, coach, hotel, church [or] public place."[28] In short, the Civil Rights Act of 1866 left the status of segregation by common carriers somewhat uncertain.

By contrast, the Civil Rights Act of 1875 specifically prohib-

---

27. *Congressional Globe,* 39th Cong., 1st sess., app. 183 (Apr. 6, 1866). To the same effect, see ibid., p. 1268 (remarks of Rep. Kerr).

28. *Germantown Telegraph,* Apr. 4, 1866, p. 3, col. 1; *Cincinnati Commercial,* Mar. 30, 1866, p. 4; ibid., Apr. 30, 1866, p. 2; Apr. 16, 1866, p. 4; Apr. 21, 1866, p. 4; *Philadelphia North American,* Apr. 10, 1866, p. 2, col. 1.

ited common carriers from segregating their cars on the basis of race. During the protracted struggle over the adoption of that statute, both Democrats and conservative Republicans raised a variety of different objections to this prohibition. Not surprisingly, Democrats generally contended that Congress could not constitutionally adopt this provision, and Republican Senator Joshua Hill of Georgia, for example, defended the right of common carriers to maintain separate but equal facilities. Taking a different tack, Republican Senators Orrin S. Ferry of Connecticut and Thomas W. Tipton of Nebraska made federalism-based arguments, complaining, that with respect to common carriers, the Sumner proposal simply duplicated existing state law. Some Republicans, however, saw the regulation of common carriers as more defensible than other portions of the proposal. For example, at the same time he argued against the regulation of juries, Senator Matthew H. Carpenter of Wisconsin declared his support for Sumner's restrictions on common carriers. Similarly, while attacking the constitutionality of most of the civil rights proposal, Senator Lot M. Morrill of Maine stated, "I have not the slightest objection that this provision should be applied to common carriers upon the national highways." Senator Lyman Trumbull of Illinois indicated that his view was similar to that of Morrill.[29] The breadth of the Republican support for the common carrier provision led to its inclusion in the statute that was finally adopted in 1875.

However, in *The Civil Rights Cases*, with only Justice John Marshall Harlan dissenting, the Supreme Court held that Congress lacked constitutional authority to prohibit common carriers from segregating passengers by race. Speaking for the Court, Justice Joseph P. Bradley treated the owners of the facilities as indistinguishable from other private parties. Bradley did not expressly reject the theory that access to common carriers, inns, and places of amusement was a basic civil right protected by the Fourteenth

---

29. *Congressional Globe*, 42d Cong., 2d sess., app. 25–29, 241–243, 892, 914, 626, app. 4, 901, 3140 (1871–72).

Amendment. Indeed, one part of his argument conceded the possibility that the Fourteenth Amendment guaranteed such access, and that Congress could require states to enforce the rights of blacks in this regard. However, Bradley concluded that Congress lacked authority to act directly against the owners of the facilities themselves. In part, this conclusion rested on a formal argument about the essential nature of rights:

> [C]ivil rights, such as are guaranteed by the constitution against state aggression, cannot be impaired by the wrongful acts of individuals, unsupported by state authority in the shape of laws, customs, or judicial or executive proceedings. The wrongful act of an individual, unsupported by any such authority, is simply a private wrong, or a crime of that individual; an invasion of the rights of the injured party, it is true... but if not sanctioned in some way by the state, or not done under state authority, his rights remain in full force, and may presumably be vindicated by resort to the laws of the state for redress.

Bradley bolstered his argument with a *Cruikshank*-like appeal to the basic concept of federalism, contending that a contrary position would allow Congress to "establish a code of municipal law regulative of all private rights between man and man in society. It would be to make congress take the place of the state legislatures and to supersede them."[30]

Harlan's dissent brought together three themes that would form the basis of his race-related jurisprudence. The first was a judicial nationalism that manifested itself in a broad definition of the powers of Congress. The second was a recognition that the freed slaves occupied a special place in constitutional analysis. The third was a relatively broad definition of fundamental rights.

---

30. 109 U.S. 3, 17, 13 (1883).

Each of these factors played an important role in his argument in *The Civil Rights Cases.*[31]

Harlan contended that the challenged provisions of the Civil Rights Act were defensible under the enforcement provisions of both the Thirteenth and Fourteenth Amendments. He began his analysis by emphasizing the need to defer to congressional judgment in most cases:

> Whether the legislative department of the government has transcended the limits of its constitutional powers "is at all times... a question of much delicacy, which ought seldom, if ever, to be decided in the affirmative in a doubtful case.... The opposition between the Constitution and the law should be such that the judge feels a clear and strong conviction of their incompatibility."..."Every possible presumption is in favor of the validity of a statute, and this continues until the contrary is shown beyond a reasonable doubt."[32]

Later in the opinion, he invoked Chief Justice John Marshall's famous language in *McCulloch v. Maryland* to support this view:

> The sound construction of the constitution must allow to the national legislature that discretion, with respect to the means by which the powers it confers are to be carried into execution, which will enable that body to perform the high duties assigned to it in the manner most beneficial to the people. Let the end be legitimate,—let it be within the scope of the con-

---

31. Loren P. Beth, *John Marshall Harlan: The Last Whig Justice* (Lexington, Ky., 1992), and Linda Przybyszewski, *The Republic According to John Marshall Harlan* (Chapel Hill, 1999), provide differing perspectives on Harlan's life and ideology.

32. *Civil Rights Cases,* 109 U.S. at 27–28 (Harlan, J., dissenting), quoting *Fletcher v. Peck*, 10 U.S. (6 Cranch.) 87, 128 (1810) and *Sinking Fund Cases*, 99 U.S. 700, 718 (1878).

> stitution,—and all means which are appropriate, which are plainly adapted to that end, which are not prohibited, but consistent with the letter and spirit of the constitution, are constitutional.[33]

From this starting point, Harlan deployed *Prigg v. Pennsylvania* against Bradley's argument that, even assuming that the rights protected by the Civil Rights Act were themselves protected by the Thirteenth and Fourteenth amendments, Congress could not act against private individuals who interfered with the ability of the freed slaves to enjoy those rights. Ironically, in relevant part, *Prigg* was a challenge to the constitutionality of the Fugitive Slave Act of 1793, which prohibited private parties from interfering with the apprehension of fugitive slaves. The source of authority for the statute was Article IV, section 2, which contains no specific enforcement language, but provides simply that "no person held to service or labor in one state, under the laws thereof, escaping into another, shall, in consequence of any law or regulation therein, be discharged from such service or labor, but shall [be returned to the master]." There, the Court rejected the claim that Congress lacked authority to pass legislation enforcing the constitutional rights of the slaveowner.

In the *Civil Rights* cases, Harlan observed that, like the Fugitive Slave Clause at issue in *Prigg*, the Thirteenth and Fourteenth amendments by their terms each provided constitutional protection for specific rights and prohibited state interference with those rights. In addition, he contended that the argument for congressional control over private action was much stronger in *The Civil Rights Cases* because, unlike the Fugitive Slave Clause, the Reconstruction amendments *expressly* provided Congress with enforcement authority. Thus, focusing specifically on the Thirteenth Amendment, he argued,

> We have seen that the power of congress, by legisla-

---

33. Ibid., p. 50, quoting *McCulloch v. Maryland*, 17 U.S. (4 Wheat.) 318, 421 (1819).

> tion, to enforce the master's right to have his slave delivered up on claim was *implied* from the recognition and guaranty of that right in the national constitution.... [More generally], [t]his court has uniformly held that the national government has the power, whether expressly given or not, to secure and protect rights conferred or guarantied by the constitution. That doctrine ought not now to be abandoned, when the inquiry is not as to an implied power to protect the master's rights, but what may congress do, under powers expressly granted, for the protection of freedom, and the rights necessarily inhering in a state of freedom.[34]

Having concluded that Congress possessed constitutional authority to criminalize private interference with the exercise of rights guaranteed by the Reconstruction amendments, Harlan next turned to a definition of those rights. He made two separate arguments, contending first that the Civil Rights Act was founded on the congressional authority to strike at the "badges and incidents" of slavery under the Thirteenth Amendment, and second that the statute was authorized by the analogous power to protect the rights guaranteed by the Fourteenth Amendment. The basic concepts underlying the two arguments were strikingly similar. Harlan juxtaposed both amendments to the decision in *Dred Scott v. Sandford*[35] and, like Justice Miller in *Slaughterhouse*, emphasized the fact that the amendments were primarily designed to ameliorate the condition of blacks in America. However, unlike Miller, Harlan saw this historical circumstance as a reason to expand the scope of federal power. Thus, while recognizing that "[t]he terms of the thirteenth amendment are absolute and universal," Harlan also noted that

34. *Civil Rights Cases,* 109 U.S. at 33–34 (Harlan, J., dissenting) (emphasis in original).

35. 60 U.S. (19 How.) 393 (1857).

> it is historically true that that amendment was suggested by the condition, of that race which had been declared by this court [in Dred Scott] to have had, according to the opinion of the white race at the time of the adoption of the constitution "no rights which the white man was bound to respect."

Conversely, Harlan noted that the Citizenship Clause of the Fourteenth Amendment "introduced all of that race, whose ancestors had been imported and sold as slaves, at once, into the political community known as the 'People of the United States.'"[36]

Harlan also saw the specific rights established by the two amendments as largely congruent. He argued that the Thirteenth Amendment protected "such civil rights as were fundamental to freedom," which he associated with "the privileges or immunities secured by [the Constitution] to citizens of the United States." Similarly, his Fourteenth Amendment argument rested on the view that section 1 had constitutionalized rights "which are fundamental in citizenship in a free government"—those protected by the Privileges and Immunities Clause of Article IV, section 2. Against this background, Harlan had little trouble in upholding the congressional ban on segregation in public conveyances and inns, emphasizing the special status of both public conveyances and inns at common law, as well as the authorities who characterized the right of access to these facilities as an inherent part of the fundamental right to "personal locomotion."[37]

Obviously, Harlan's defeat in *The Civil Rights Cases* dealt a severe blow to efforts to desegregate the nation's transportation system. However, even Bradley's opinion at least strongly implied that any attempt by the state to *require* segregation in these facilities would still be held unconstitutional. In fact, *Hall v. DeCuir*[38]—a case decided before *The Civil Rights Cases*—seemed

---

36. *Civil Rights Cases,* 109 U.S. at 33, 46 (Harlan, J., dissenting).
37. Ibid., pp. 33, 47, 37–41.
38. 95 U.S. 485 (1877).

to suggest that, at least in some circumstances, any such state mandate would face severe constitutional difficulties beyond those posed by the Reconstruction amendments themselves.

Hall did not involve a state law requiring carriers to provide separate facilities for the races; instead, it was an attack on a Louisiana statute that *forbade* racial segregation by those transporting passengers within the state. A Fourteenth Amendment challenge to this statute was almost unthinkable; instead, the owner of a steamboat engaged in interstate traffic argued that the state requirement ran afoul of the dormant Commerce Clause. In unanimously striking down the statute, the Court characterized the requirement as a "direct burden upon inter-state commerce," arguing that "while [the statute] purports only to control the carrier when engaged within the State, it must necessarily influence his conduct to some extent in the management of his business throughout his entire voyage." Noting the difficulties that might arise if other states in which the steamboat operated passed statutes requiring segregation, the Court concluded that "commerce cannot flourish in the midst of such embarrassments" and that "uniformity in the regulations by which [the interstate traffic in passengers] is to be governed . . . is a necessity . . . and to secure it Congress, which is untrammeled by State lines, has been invested with the exclusive legislative power of determining what such regulations shall be."[39]

This analysis—consistent with other dormant Commerce Clause decisions of the same era—clearly implied that no state could adopt any regulation that either required or prohibited racial segregation by interstate carriers. The race-related nature of the regulation was not, however, critical to the decision. Instead, the *Hall* Court analogized the Louisiana statute to other barriers to the free flow of interstate commerce. The logic of the decision was therefore inherently self-limiting.

This point was soon made clear in *Louisville Railway Co. v.*

---

39. Ibid., pp. 488–489.

Mississippi. *Louisville Railway* was a dormant Commerce Clause challenge to a Mississippi statute that required carriers to maintain separate but equal facilities for passengers of different races. A majority of the Court rejected this challenge, distinguishing *Hall* on the ground that the Mississippi courts had limited the applicability of the *Louisville Railway* statute to intrastate traffic. Thus, the majority concluded that the limitations imposed on the states by the Commerce Clause were not implicated. Justices Harlan and Bradley took a different view of the statute,[40] arguing that it applied to all trains operating within the state—even those engaged in interstate commerce. From this perspective, they saw the case as indistinguishable from *Hall*, declaring, "It is difficult to understand how a state enactment, requiring the separation of the white and black races on interstate carriers of passengers, is [not] a regulation of commerce among the states, while a similar enactment forbidding such separation is . . . a regulation of that character."[41]

Of course, *Louisville Railway* did not end the controversy over the constitutionality of state-imposed racial segregation in public transportation. While rejecting one line of attack, the majority in that case expressly refused to foreclose other potential constitutional challenges. The Court noted that because the action had been initiated by the railroad itself rather than by an individual passenger, "there is not question of personal insult or alleged violation of personal rights."[42] Thus, *Louisville Railway* left open the possibility that the Mississippi regulation might be held to violate the Fourteenth Amendment.

It was against this background that *Plessy v. Ferguson*[43] was decided. In *Plessy*, the Court considered the constitutionality of a Louisiana statute that required railroads to maintain separate but

40. 133 U.S. 592–594 (1890).

41. Ibid., pp. 589, 589–590 (1890); ibid., pp. 592–594 (Bradley, J., dissenting).

42. Ibid., p. 589.

43. 163 U.S. 537 (1896).

equal accommodations for the "white and colored races" and to enforce the segregation of the races. The statute was challenged by a man of mixed racial background who was refused the right to sit in the car reserved for white passengers. By a 7-1 margin, the Fuller Court upheld the constitutionality of the Louisiana statute.

Speaking for the majority, Justice Henry B. Brown first rejected a Thirteenth Amendment challenge to the statute, declaring, "A statute which implies merely a legal distinction between the races... has no tendency to destroy the legal equality of the two races, or re-establish a state of involuntary servitude."[44] Turning to the Fourteenth Amendment, Brown began by sketching in general terms his vision of the reach of the amendment:

> The object of the amendment was undoubtedly to enforce the absolute equality of the two races before the law, but in the nature of things it could not have been intended to abolish distinctions based upon color, as distinguished from political equality, or a commingling of the two races upon grounds unsatisfactory to either.[45]

The key question, of course, was how one was to define the phrase "equality... before the law." In part, Brown's treatment of this issue reflected the evolution of the Republican position on race during the Reconstruction era. As has already been noted, at the time the Fourteenth Amendment was drafted, many Republicans drew a sharp distinction between civil rights and political rights, and the drafters made a conscious decision not to directly protect political rights. For Brown, by contrast, political equality was an essential element of equality before the law, and he cited the jury discrimination struck down in *Strauder v. West Virginia* as the classic example of a forbidden racial classification. Outside the area of political rights, however, Brown was far more willing

---

44. Ibid., p. 543.
45. Ibid., pp. 543, 543–544.

to countenance the use of race in government decision-making. He cited a series of state court decisions that had upheld school segregation as a paradigm for the view that some racially based laws did not violate Fourteenth Amendment principles.[46]

Having established the parameters of his analysis, Brown next turned to the case law that had dealt specifically with the issue of segregation by common carriers, concluding that the right of access to public conveyances did not merit special constitutional protection. He then applied a rational basis test, noting that "every exercise of the police power must be reasonable, and extend only to such laws as are enacted for the promotion of the public good, and not for the annoyance or oppression of a particular class." Characterizing the Louisiana statute as an appropriate measure to ensure "good order" and the comfort of passengers of all races, Brown then proceeded to the most widely quoted portion of his opinion:

> We consider the underlying fallacy of the plaintiff's argument to consist in the assumption that the enforced separation of the two races stamps the colored race with a badge of inferiority. If this be so, it is not by reason of anything found in the act, but solely because the colored race chooses to put that construction upon it.... Legislation is powerless to eradicate racial instincts or to abolish distinctions based upon physical differences, and the attempt to do so can only result in accentuating the difficulties of the present situation. If the civil and political rights of both races be equal one cannot be inferior to the other civilly or politically. If one race be inferior to the other socially, the Constitution of the United States cannot put them on the same plane.[47]

---

46. Ibid., pp. 544–545. The leading case in this line was *Roberts v. City of Boston*, 59 Mass. (5 Cush.) 198 (1849), discussed in chapter 1.

47. *Plessy*, 163 U.S. at 550, 551–552.

Justice Harlan's dissenting opinion, with its ringing endorsement of the view that "[o]ur Constitution is color-blind, and neither knows nor tolerates classes among citizens,"[48] is normally juxtaposed with Brown's treatment of the claim that the Louisiana statute did not imply that blacks were an inferior race. Such comparisons obscure a crucial difference in the contexts of the two statements. Harlan was not addressing the reasonableness of the statute. Indeed, he explicitly disclaimed the notion that the classification could be invalidated simply because the Court found it "unreasonable."[49] Instead, Harlan saw the Louisiana statute as denying rights that even the majority in *The Civil Rights Cases* had suggested that the states were under a constitutional obligation to protect.

Harlan's position in *Plessy* was thus nothing more than a logical extension of his *Civil Rights* dissent. There, his argument for federal power had been premised on the view that the right to be free from segregation on common carriers was a fundamental right protected by the Fourteenth amendment, and that therefore, Congress had authority to secure that right directly by legislation. Given that position, he could hardly countenance a state statute that explicitly violated that right. Against this background, it should not be surprising that many aspects of Harlan's *Plessy* dissent bear striking similarities to his *Civil Rights* opinion. As in *The Civil Rights Cases,* Harlan linked the Thirteenth and Fourteenth amendments to "a common purpose, namely, to secure 'to a race recently emancipated, a race that through many generations have been held in slavery, all the civil rights that the superior may enjoy.'"[50] Moreover, once again, his argument emphasized the fundamental nature of the right at issue; indeed, the *Plessy* dissent begins, not with a condemnation of race discrimination generally, but rather with a renewed demonstration of the

---

48. Ibid., p. 559.
49. Ibid., pp. 559, 558–559 (Harlan, J., dissenting).
50. Ibid., p. 556, citing *Strauder,* 100 U.S. at 306, 307.

special status of public railways at common law[51]—a demonstration that, later in the opinion, Harlan once again linked to Blackstone's right of "personal locomotion." In addition, although he analogized the case to *Strauder*,[52] Harlan was careful to limit his invocations of the principle of color-blindness to situations involving "civil rights," those which he saw as "common to all citizens,"[53] concluding, "The arbitrary separation of citizens, while they are on a public highway, is a badge of servitude wholly inconsistent with the civil freedom and the equality before the law established by the Constitution."[54] Thus, by its terms, Harlan's opinion left open the possibility that he might view other state-imposed racial classifications as constitutional.[55] Indeed, in 1883, he had already implicitly countenanced a racial classification in *Pace v. Alabama*, and in 1899 he would strongly suggest that he viewed the maintenance of segregated schools as constitutional.[56]

---

51. Ibid., p. 554.
52. Ibid., pp. 557–558.
53. Ibid., p. 554.
54. Ibid., p. 562.
55. Owen M. Fiss, *Troubled Beginnings of the Modern State, 1888–1910* (New York, 1993), pp. 362–370, also emphasizes the importance of the concept of fundamental rights to Harlan's analysis in *Plessy*.
56. Ibid., pp. 554, 557–558, 554, 552; *Pace v. Alabama*, 103 U.S. 583 (1883); *Cumming v. County Board of Election*, 175 U.S. 528 (1899).

Pace was a challenge to the sentencing provisions of an Alabama statute punishing "adultery [and] fornication." If the parties engaging in the prohibited acts were members of the same race, the punishment for the first offense was imprisonment for not more than six months. If, however, one of the parties was white and the other black, the punishment was imprisonment for between two and seven years. Harlan concurred silently in Justice Stephen Field's opinion rejecting an equal protection challenge to the sentencing provisions. Field reasoned that where either intraracial or interracial acts were involved, the blacks and whites engaged in the acts were subject to the same penalties. Thus, he concluded, "the discrimination... made in the punishment is directed against the offence designated and not against the person of any particular color or race." *Pace*, 103 U.S. at 585.

For a detailed analysis of *Cumming*, see J. Morgan Kousser, "Separate but Not Equal: The Supreme Court's First Decision on Racial Discrimination in Schools," *Journal of Southern History* 46 (1980): 17–44.

In short, the available evidence indicates that Harlan was less committed to a modern vision of racial equality than many commentators have suggested. Instead, he seems to have adhered to the vision of limited absolute equality that animated Republican political theory for much of the nineteenth century. Conversely, the views of Henry Billings Brown and those who joined his opinion in *Plessy* were the product of a different political culture. Only Stephen Field had been a member of the *Strauder* Court, and he had authored a vigorous dissent. Most of the justices had been appointed in the 1890s—the period in which even the Republican party was in full retreat from its historic commitment to the protection of African Americans. Thus, *Plessy* exemplifies the impact of political change on the evolution of constitutional doctrine.

Chapter 7

Conclusion

Scholars often understate the complexity of the forces that shaped the early judicial interpretation of the Reconstruction amendments. Most standard accounts describe the late-nineteenth-century case law as almost entirely a product of conservative political thought. In fact, however, the forces that shaped the law of the Reconstruction amendments in the late nineteenth century are a microcosm of those that impact the development of constitutional law more generally. Like most of those who draft constitutional provisions, the framers of the Reconstruction amendments had clear expectations of the legal import of the language that they chose. The drafters were often successful in establishing the general direction of the law; however, the legal doctrines that were derived from the amendments were also profoundly influenced by the idiosyncratic views of the justices of the Supreme Court and the political context that provided the background for their decisions.

Some of the Court's decisions clearly reflected the influence of distinctively legal analysis. *Wong Kim Ark* is perhaps the most prominent example of such a decision. Given the rampant anti-Chinese prejudice of late-nineteenth-century American society, conservative ideology would clearly have mandated a rejection of the claim that Wong Kim Ark was a United States citizen. Nonetheless, a majority of the justices took the view that he did in fact have a right to claim American citizenship. Such a result is only explicable in terms of distinctively legal analysis.

Strauder provides an even more striking example of the rejection of conservative political values. There, turning aside both the understanding of those who drafted the Reconstruction amendments and the import of equal protection language in the antebellum legal culture, the Court introduced a novel concept into mainstream constitutional jurisprudence—the idea that racial discrimination was per se suspect. Admittedly, other legal doctrines sharply limited the immediate practical impact of the *Strauder* decision. Nonetheless, its long-term significance would be difficult to overstate. Indeed, it is hardly an exaggeration to suggest that the entire structure of post-*Brown* jurisprudence, with its emphasis on suspect and quasi-suspect classifications, is based on the principles first enunciated in *Strauder.*

These decisions suggest the need for a reevaluation of the Court's performance in the late nineteenth century. They simply cannot be squared with accounts that describe the Court during this period as an unflinchingly reactionary institution. To be sure, the Court's actions in *The Slaughterhouse Cases, United States v. Cruikshank, The Civil Rights Cases,* and *Plessy v. Ferguson* are appropriately characterized as by-products of conservative political ideology. However, *Wong Kim Ark* and *Strauder* clearly reflect the influence of other forces. Against this background, the characterization of the case law as unremittingly conservative is not only unflattering; it is also unfair.

Index